STRATEGIC
STUDIES
INSTITUTE

The Strategic Studies Institute (SSI) is part of the U.S. Army War College and is the strategic-level study agent for issues related to national security and military strategy with emphasis on geostrategic analysis.

The mission of SSI is to use independent analysis to conduct strategic studies that develop policy recommendations on:

- Strategy, planning, and policy for joint and combined employment of military forces;

- Regional strategic appraisals;

- The nature of land warfare;

- Matters affecting the Army's future;

- The concepts, philosophy, and theory of strategy; and,

- Other issues of importance to the leadership of the Army.

Studies produced by civilian and military analysts concern topics having strategic implications for the Army, the Department of Defense, and the larger national security community.

In addition to its studies, SSI publishes special reports on topics of special or immediate interest. These include edited proceedings of conferences and topically oriented roundtables, expanded trip reports, and quick-reaction responses to senior Army leaders.

The Institute provides a valuable analytical capability within the Army to address strategic and other issues in support of Army participation in national security policy formulation.

i

Strategic Studies Institute
and
U.S. Army War College Press

RUSSIA AND THE CASPIAN SEA: PROJECTING POWER OR COMPETING FOR INFLUENCE?

Tracey German

August 2014

*****

Comments pertaining to this report are invited and should be forwarded to: Director, Strategic Studies Institute and U.S. Army War College Press, U.S. Army War College, 47 Ashburn Drive, Carlisle, PA 17013-5010.

*****

This manuscript was funded by the U.S. Army War College External Research Associates Program. Information on this program is available on our website, *www.StrategicStudies Institute.army.mil*, at the Opportunities tab.

*****

*****

The Strategic Studies Institute and U.S. Army War College Press publishes a monthly email newsletter to update the national security community on the research of our analysts, recent and forthcoming publications, and upcoming conferences sponsored by the Institute. Each newsletter also provides a strategic commentary by one of our research analysts. If you are interested in receiving this newsletter, please subscribe on the SSI website at *www.StrategicStudiesInstitute.army.mil/newsletter*.

FOREWORD

In November 2012, Russia's Caspian Flotilla celebrated its 290th anniversary. Established by Peter the Great in 1722, the Flotilla was a key component of the Russian Empire's expansion into the Caspian region, and nearly 300 years later, it remains a vital element of continued Russian influence in its "south." The Caspian Sea and the "south" have been fundamental to Russian security since the 18th century, when imperial Russia needed to secure and maintain trade links with the Persian Empire, as well as prevent any further Persian encroachment. Growing rivalry between Russia and its imperial competitors in the Caucasus and Central Asia in the 18th and 19th centuries led to frequent military clashes in the Caspian Sea, giving the Caspian Flotilla renewed military significance. The drivers of international interest in the Caspian Sea have changed little since the 18th century, and historical events have resonance with the contemporary situation: the competition for influence between different regional powers; the region's geostrategic significance, with Iran lying directly to the south; the vital importance of economic factors; maintaining access to natural resources, as well as lucrative trade routes; and the influence of external actors on the development of the region.

Moscow's concerns in the Caspian region reflect wider concerns about growing U.S. (and European) influence in areas traditionally perceived as Russia's "strategic backyard," in states such as Georgia, Ukraine, and the Central Asian republics—concern that is reflected in key Russian strategic documents, including the 2008 *Foreign Policy Concept*, 2009 *National Security Strategy*, and 2010 *Military Doctrine*. Russian political discourse focuses on the former Soviet space as a sphere of its exclusive influence, or, as Russian President Dmitry Medvedev has put it, Russia's "zone of privileged interest," and Moscow has sought to counterbalance the growing involvement of other actors in the region. Russian policies vis-à-vis former Soviet states in Central Asia, the South Caucasus, and its Western periphery (Ukraine, Moldova, and Belarus) in the contemporary era are focused on maintaining influence and protecting Russia's interests. The "influence" narrative reflects Russia's desire to reassert itself across the former Soviet space in order to counter the perceived expansion of Western involvement, particularly North Atlantic Treaty Organization enlargement, within its "sphere of influence." Events in Ukraine in 2014 (and Georgia in 2008) emphasize the crucial importance of having a clear understanding of how Russia views the growing influence of external actors within its "zone of privileged interest" and the impact on its relations with states in what is considered to be its "near abroad."

DOUGLAS C. LOVELACE, JR.
Director
Strategic Studies Institute and
    U.S. Army War College Press

ABOUT THE AUTHOR

TRACEY GERMAN is a senior lecturer in the Defence Studies Department at King's College London, United Kingdom (UK), which provides postgraduate-level teaching at the UK's Joint Services Command and Staff College (JSCSC). Her research focuses on Russia's relations with its neighbors, military reform, energy issues, as well as conflict and security in the Caucasus and Caspian region. Dr. German has published widely on intra- and interstate conflicts in the region, notably Nagorno-Karabakh, Chechnya, South Ossetia, and Abkhazia. Publications include *Regional Cooperation in the South Caucasus: Good Neighbours or Distant Relatives?* (Ashgate Publishing Ltd., 2012), *Russia's Chechen War* (Routledge, 2003), and co-authored *Securing Europe: Western Interventions towards a New Security Community* (IB Tauris, 2009), as well as articles in journals such as *European Security, Europe-Asia Studies, Small Wars and Insurgencies, Central Asian Survey, Vestnik analitiki*, and *Politique étrangère*.

SUMMARY

This monograph examines Russia's policy toward the Caspian Sea region as Moscow attempts to counterbalance growing American involvement within what it perceives to be its zone of privileged interest, focusing on the recent expansion of the Caspian Flotilla and the rationale behind it. Moscow has sought to counterbalance the growing involvement of other actors in the region, which has led to rising tension between Russia and its southern neighbors. The primary objectives of the research are to examine Russian perceptions of threat and security in the Caspian region and assess the implications for other actors. This monograph analyzes the drivers of the increasing competition for influence, focusing on developments within the energy sector, and assess the implications of Russia's consolidation of its dominance for security and stability in the region. This issue is important because a clear understanding of Russian strategic thinking and threat perception in the Caspian Sea is vital in order to facilitate effective U.S. policy in the wider Caucasus and Central Asian region.

RUSSIA AND THE CASPIAN SEA: PROJECTING POWER OR COMPETING FOR INFLUENCE?

In November 2012, Russia's Caspian Flotilla celebrated its 290th anniversary. Established by Peter the Great in 1722, the Flotilla was a key component of the Russian Empire's expansion into the Caspian region, and nearly 300 years later, it remains a vital element of continued Russian influence in its "south." The Russian Ministry of Defense (MOD) describes the Caspian Flotilla as "not only the southernmost outpost of Russia, but also the guarantor of the integrity of maritime boundaries and the most important foreign policy tool of the state in the Caspian Sea."[1] The Flotilla has recovered from the collapse of the Union of Soviet Socialist Republics (USSR) in 1991 and its subsequent redeployment from Baku to Astrakhan. Unlike other Russian fleets, it has not been reduced in size, but has been the focus of significant investment in recent years. By 2020, the Caspian Flotilla will have received as many as 16 new vessels, a striking number for a relatively small, "closed" basin with no access to the open seas, where the littoral states control access in and out of the region. This raises questions about Russian perceptions of threat and security in the Caspian region: who and/or what does Russia perceive to be such a security challenge in the area that it needs to upgrade its naval capabilities so significantly?

The Caspian Sea is part of Russia's "southern underbelly" (*yuzhnaya podbryush"ye*[2]), a term that underscores the sense of vulnerability Russia feels along its southern border. Rich in resources, the broader Caspian region is also an area of ongoing border disputes, transnational threats, and growing international

1

interest. The region's geographic location confers both important advantages and a number of challenges: The development of international transport and communication corridors across the Sea are undoubtedly an advantage, although this is countered by the fact that Azerbaijan, Kazakhstan, and Turkmenistan are landlocked and reliant upon other countries to export their hydrocarbons to international markets. Furthermore, the key strategic location of the Caspian, linking Asia and Europe, and the lack of consensus among the five littoral states about the legal status of the Sea, facilitate the passage of security challenges such as international terrorism, illegal migration, transnational organized crime, and trafficking from Central Asia to Europe.

Russia traditionally has been the biggest regional power and, despite the appearance of new actors within the region in the wake of the breakup of the USSR that challenged Russian hegemony, it remains the principal economic and military power in the Caspian region, largely a result of historical legacy. Moscow considers the region to be a sphere of its exclusive influence, or, as former Russian President Dmitry Medvedev has put it, Russia's "zone of privileged interest," and has sought to counterbalance the growing involvement of other actors. Thus, Russian policies vis-à-vis the Caspian region (and the wider former Soviet area) are focused on maintaining influence and protecting its political and economic interests in the region. Former Soviet states are generally wary of pursuing policies that run counter to Russian interests, limiting the ability of other actors, such as the United States, to increase their cooperation with these states. The region is unique in terms of Russia's relations with its neighbors within the wider "south," as it contains three former Soviet states, none of which is willing to remain wholly dependent on Moscow (as, for example, Armenia is), but which have also been unwilling to turn their backs on Russia (as Georgia has tried to do). Both Azerbaijan and Kazakhstan have sought to balance their relations with Russia against deepening cooperation with the West in order to maintain their independence, while Turkmenistan pursues a policy of "Positive Neutrality" in its foreign relations. The final littoral state, Iran, is an historic rival of Russia. It considers itself to be a regional power and has substantial historical, cultural, and ethnic links with neighboring states in the region, inherited from the Persian Empire, which complicate its foreign relations. Nevertheless, although it is a rival for influence, Iran also shares a common desire with Russia to counter the increasing presence of external powers in region, particularly the United States.

The rise in U.S. (and European) interests in the Caspian region over the past decade has led to rising tension between Russia and its southern neighbors. The United States views the Caspian as an important strategic arena: as well as its geostrategic location, with Iran lying directly to the south, it is a significant source of hydrocarbons. It has become increasingly important to the economic security of the West as international oil companies have spent vast sums of money on exploration and development there, particularly in Azerbaijan and Kazakhstan. However, limited export options, as well as reliance upon the Russian pipeline network and neighboring countries, have restricted the ability of countries in the Caspian to profit fully from their extensive oil and gas reserves. Consequently, there has been considerable investment in new international export pipelines

3

over the past decade, undermining Russian influence. Some Russian observers have described the issue of pipelines in the landlocked Caspian region as a "battle for domination," particularly on the part of the United States, which "is seeking to accelerate the process of the political and economic isolation of former Soviet republics from Russia."[3] While this view ascribes little autonomy of action to the states involved, it does highlight the suspicion with which Moscow regards growing Western (particularly U.S.) influence in the Caspian region.[4]

The Caspian Sea has also been playing a vital role in the logistics operation to support the International Security Assistance Force (ISAF) in Afghanistan. It forms part of the southern route of the Northern Distribution Network (NDN), which was established in 2009 to move troop supplies into Afghanistan, avoiding the hazardous route through Pakistan. By 2011, the NDN handled about 40 percent of Afghanistan-bound traffic, compared to 30 percent through Pakistan. The southern route starts at the Georgian Black Sea port of Poti, crossing the Caucasus to Baku in Azerbaijan, where goods are then ferried across the Caspian Sea to Kazakhstan and then moved by rail or truck through Uzbekistan to the Afghan border. This route carries approximately one-third of the NDN's traffic. Kazakhstan has been seeking to develop its port of Aqtau on the Caspian Sea and turn it into a major regional transit hub. As the country's only seaport and described as the "sea-gate to a sovereign Kazakhstan,"[5] Aqtau has played a key role in the ISAF logistics chain and is set to grow in importance as the United States and other ISAF contributors withdraw from Afghanistan in 2014. Reports in the Russian media suggested that the United States may establish a transhipment point at Aqtau, as a means of getting its military equipment out of Afghanistan and highlighted Russian opposition to the presence of any external actors in the closed system of the Caspian Sea. An article in *Nezavisimaya Gazeta* argued that, if Aqtau became a base for "the Pentagon and its allies," the "already fragile Caspian security architecture would effectively collapse."[6] Moscow has tolerated limited U.S. military support for Azerbaijan and Kazakhstan in terms of training and equipment support through the Caspian Guard initiative. However, the prospect of the potential establishment of a transhipment base at Aqtau appears to be a step too far for Russia (and Iran) and could lead to growth in tension in the area.

This monograph examines Russia's policy toward the Caspian Sea region as Moscow attempts to counterbalance growing American involvement within what it perceives to be its zone of privileged interest, focusing on the recent expansion of the Caspian Flotilla and the rationale behind it. The primary objectives of the research are to analyze Russian perceptions of threat and security in the Caspian region and assess the implications for other actors. It will assess the importance of the "south" to Russian perceptions of security and analyze whether U.S./Western influence in the Caspian region is viewed as a security challenge by Moscow. What steps have been taken since 1991 to develop any form of regional security system and what has been Russia's role in this? The monograph focuses on developments within the energy sector and assesses the implications of Russia's consolidation of its dominance for energy security and stability in the region. This issue is important because a clear understanding of Russian strategic thinking and threat perception in the Caspian Sea is vital in order to facilitate effective U.S. policy in the region and avoid a repeat of the events of 2008 in Georgia.

THE CASPIAN SEA AND ITS SIGNIFICANCE

According to some sources, over the centuries the Caspian Sea has been known by more than 50 different names.[7] At various times, the ancient Persians called it the Hyrcanian and Persian Sea, while old Russian documents refer to it as the Khvalin Sea, after the Khvali people that inhabited the area. Other names given to the Sea have included Avar, Baku, Apsheron, and Khazar. The name "Caspian" is thought to be derived from the name of an ancient tribe that lived on the southwest shore of the Sea, the Caspi people.[8] Russian interest in the Caspian began in earnest during the 17th century with the development of trade links with Persia, which led to an expansion of shipping routes along the Volga river and down across the Caspian Sea. The growing Russian empire needed the abundant natural resources found in and around the Sea, as well as the trade links between east and west and routes across the Caspian. This stimulated the need for the development of a Russian naval capability to protect its commercial interests in the region, and Tsar Alexis I ordered the construction of naval ships. The *Oryel* was the first Russian warship to be constructed; it set sail for Astrakhan in 1669, under the command of Dutch captain David Butler.[9]

During the 18th century Russia sought to dominate the area, leading to the development of its own Caspian naval flotilla. Established by Peter the Great in 1722, the flotilla was a key component of the Russian Empire's expansion in the Caspian region. Russia was becoming increasingly concerned about growing rivalry with both the Ottoman and Persian Empires in the southwest Caspian and Caucasus.[10] As the empire grew, it had come into conflict with the other imperial powers in the region, the Ottomans and Persians. The competition for territory and resources in the 18th and 19th centuries led to frequent military clashes on the Caspian Sea, giving the Caspian Flotilla renewed military significance. Moscow was determined to maintain its lucrative trade routes and defend its allies in the region, a state of affairs that has resonance with the contemporary situation.

There are significant similarities between historical events and contemporary circumstances in the region, and the drivers of international interest in the Caspian Sea have changed little since the 18th century: the competition for influence between different regional powers, the region's geostrategic significance, with Iran lying directly to the south; the vital importance of economic factors and maintaining access to natural resources; as well as lucrative trade routes and concern about the influence of external actors on the development of the region. Over the past decade, the region has grown in further significance within the contemporary security environment, particularly its political, strategic, and economic importance for Western security. International oil companies have spent vast sums of money on exploration and development in the wider Caspian region, and the Sea has become an important transit route for the ISAF logistics operation. Rich in resources and lying on a key East-West transit route, the Caspian has attracted considerable international (particularly U.S.) interest over the past decade, triggering rising tension between Russia and its southern neighbors. Russia traditionally has been the biggest regional power, and its ties to the region remain strong. Moscow considers the broader Caspian region to be a sphere of its exclusive influence, and it is unhappy about the growing influence of other external actors such as the United States, Europe, Turkey, and Iran, which, since 1991, has posed a direct challenge to Russian hegemony in the region.

The Caspian Sea is also where imperial Russia began to develop naval vessels for the purpose of defending its national and commercial interests during the 17th and 18th centuries, leading to the development of a navy. Russia's current maritime doctrine, approved in 2001 and looking out to 2020, describes the navy as an "instrument of foreign policy . . . intended to protect the interests of the Russian Federation and its allies."[11] It goes on to describe Russia as "historically . . . a leading maritime power," a consequence of the country's "spatial and geophysical attributes," and identifies the Caspian as a unique region in terms of the "volume and quantity" of its mineral and bio-resources. This is reflected in the role of the Caspian Flotilla which, in addition to protecting Russian shipping, also provides protection to Russian offshore hydrocarbon production facilities against potential threats and monitors the extraction of hydrocarbons and bio-resources (such as sturgeon) in disputed areas of the Sea. The objectives of Russian maritime policy in the Caspian Sea region are:

- The establishment of a legal regime in the Caspian Sea that is favorable for Russia in terms of exploiting resources such as fish stocks and hydrocarbons;
- Protecting the marine environment in cooperation with the other littoral states;
- Creating the conditions for basing and utilization of all naval/maritime potential;

- Renewal of merchant, combined (river-sea) and fishing fleets;
- Preventing displacement of Russian fleet from maritime transport market;
- Organization of ferry services as part of "inter-modal" transport network with access to the Mediterranean and Baltic Seas; and,
- Development, reconstruction, and specialization of existing ports.[12]

This monograph uses these maritime policy objectives, particularly the first three, as a framework to analyze the significance of the Caspian Sea region for Russia and further understand the motivations for the expansion and capability upgrade of the Caspian Flotilla. It begins with an appraisal of the Sea's resources, both hydrocarbons and sturgeon, before examining cooperation and obstacles to cooperation between the littoral states, the importance of the Sea for Russian security, and the development of naval capabilities there.

CASPIAN RESOURCES

Oil and Gas Reserves.

The Caspian Sea was the site of the world's first commercial oil industry, with the development of oil reserves in Azerbaijan (then part of the Russian Empire) at the end of the 19th century. Following the collapse of the Soviet Union in 1991, the Caspian region was heralded as the Middle East of the future because of its potential hydrocarbon reserves. However, the euphoria and optimism that accompanied the initial involvement of foreign investors in the region has been tempered by difficult operating conditions, both political and geological. Although the Caspian has been lauded as the new Middle East, current proven reserves indicate a greater similarity with the North Sea than with the Persian Gulf (see Table 1).

	Proven Oil Reserves (Billion Barrels)	Share of Global Total Percent	Reserve-to-Production (R/P) Ratio	Proven Gas Reserves (Trillion Cubic Meters)	Share of Global Total Percent	R/P Ratio
Azerbaijan	7.0	0.4	21.9	0.9	0.5	57.1
Kazakhstan	30.0	1.8	47.4	1.3	0.7	65.6
Russia	87.2	5.2	22.4	32.9	17.6	55.6
Turkmenistan	0.6	-	7.4	17.5	9.3	-
Saudi Arabia	265.9	15.9	63	8.2	4.4	80.1
Iran	157	9.4	-	33.6	18.0	-

Table 1. Comparison of Proved Reserves in the Caspian and Middle East, 2012.[13]

The North and South Caspian Basins are very different. The North is comprised of shallow waters, which are ice-bound during the winter months, presenting a serious technical challenge for energy companies. It is also the location of sturgeon breeding grounds. The South is deeper, but is not thought to contain as much oil and is possibly more gas-prone. Exploratory drilling in the South Caspian Basin has significantly reduced estimates of future oil potential and foreign companies have begun to adopt a more moderate attitude toward the development of the Caspian's hydrocarbon reserves. In terms of hydrocarbon resources, oil reserves are predominantly concentrated in Western Kazakhstan and the Caspian Sea, with large natural gas reserves found in Turkmenistan, Uzbekistan, and Kazakhstan.

Kazakhstan, where oil was first discovered over 100 years ago, has the largest recoverable reserves of oil in the Caspian Sea region. According to British Petroleum's (BP) *Statistical Review of World Energy,* published in 2013, the country has proven oil reserves of 30 billion barrels and was producing 1.7 million barrels per day (bpd) in 2012, making it a major producer. Kazakhstan's proven natural gas reserves stood at 1.3 Trillion cubic meters (Tcm) in 2012, the majority of which are located in the west of the country. According to the U.S. Energy Information Agency (EIA), around 80 percent of the country's total natural gas reserves are found in just four fields: Karachaganak, Tengiz, Imashevskoye, and Kashagan.

Oil is located primarily in the west of the country, both on- and offshore. Current production is dominated by two giant onshore fields, Tengiz and Karachaganak, which together produced over 40 percent of the country's total output in 2013.[14] Tengiz is Kazakhstan's largest field, with daily production of over 500,000 bpd. It is operated by Tengizchevroil (TCO), a joint venture that includes major U.S. oil companies Chevron and ExxonMobil, together with KazMunaiGaz and LukArco.[15] Karachaganak accounted for around 12 percent of the total oil production in 2013. Its operator, Karachaganak Petroleum Operating (KPO), includes BG, ENI, Chevron and LUKoil.[16]

It is estimated that two-thirds of future oil production will be from the North Caspian Basin, predominantly from the giant offshore Kashagan field being developed by the North Caspian Operating Company (NCOC) consortium, comprising KazMunaiGaz, Shell, ENI, ExxonMobil, Total, Inpex, and the China National Petroleum Corporation (CNPC). Kashagan is thought to be one of the largest known fields outside of the Middle East and has been described as the "world's largest oil discovery in 5 decades."[17] It is hoped that it will provide a reliable indicator of the Caspian's potential oil supply: exploratory drilling has indicated that the field holds up to 35 billion barrels of oil, of which approximately 25 percent (7-9 billion barrels) can be produced. Production has been delayed several times, largely because of extreme operating conditions. The first production is expected in the spring of 2014, with production being increased from 180,000 bpd during the first phase to as much as 370,000 bpd in the second. Located in shallow waters that freeze in winter, damaging equipment and making maintenance difficult, the field also produces toxic hydrogen sulphide. A gas leak in October 2013 led to a further halt in operations and raised concerns about potential environmental damage. The development of Kazakhstan's "superfields" is key to the country's long-term economic growth, and Kashagan in particular is vital for the country to achieve its goal of increasing crude oil output by 60 percent by the end of the decade. Kashagan is the only offshore "superfield" and therefore the only one currently with direct relevance to the Caspian Sea.

In September 2013, China's CNPC acquired an 8.33 percent stake in the Kashagan consortium for U.S.$5 billion.[18] The purchase was part of a series of deals signed by Chinese President Xi Jingping[19] during a tour of Central Asia to secure access to the region's hydrocarbons and was symbolic of the increasing Chinese presence in the region. The deal was also indicative of the competition for influence occurring in the region, particularly over access to hydrocarbons: CNPC beat its Indian rival Oil and Natural Gas Company (ONGC) to the stake, which was held by U.S.

12

major oil company, ConocoPhillips, until July 2013. Kazakhstan's extensive hydrocarbon reserves have stimulated a lot of international interest and increased the presence of external actors in the Caspian region, undermining Russian influence. While the country has so far managed to balance successfully its relations with Moscow, the West, and Beijing, their conflicting interests and notions of security could undermine stability in the medium to long term, and Kazakhstan will need to develop its naval forces to be able to demonstrate its intent to protect its interests in the Caspian Sea.

Azerbaijan's sector of the Caspian Sea also contains significant hydrocarbon reserves, although there are indications that it may be more gas- than oil-prone. Recent exploration in the Azeri sector of the Caspian Sea has been disappointing, with the exception of the BP-led Azeri-Chirag-Guneshli (ACG) superstructure, and several wells have been plugged. Azerbaijan's proven crude oil reserves were estimated at 7 billion barrels in 2012 (see Table 1). The country's largest hydrocarbon basins are located offshore, with the majority of its oil currently being produced from the ACG fields. The U.S.$8 billion deal, which established the BP-led Azerbaijan International Operating Corporation to develop the Azeri, Chirag, and Guneshli offshore fields, was concluded in 1994. Dubbed the "contract of the century," it was the Azeri government's first international oil agreement with a consortium of global oil companies and marked Azerbaijan's entrance onto the international energy market. The ACG concession is the largest international project in Azerbaijan and comprises three fields with total reserves estimated to be at least 5.4 billion barrels of recoverable oil.[20] Azerbaijan's total oil production was expected to peak by 2012, and recent data suggests that production has been declining over the past couple of years (see Table 2).

	Oil Production (barrels per day)	Year-on-Year Change Percent	Share of Global Total Percent	Gas Production (Billion cubic meters)	Year-on-Year Change Percent	Share of Global Total Percent
Azerbaijan	872,000	-5.2	1.1	15.6	+5.1	0.5
Kazakhstan	1,728,000	-1.6	2.0	19.7	+2.0	0.6
Russia	10,643,000	+1.2	12.8	592.3	-2.7	17.6
Turkmenistan	222,000	+2.5	0.3	64.4	+7.8	1.9
Saudi Arabia	11,530,000	+3.7	13.3	102.8	+11.1	3.0
Iran	3,680,000	-16.2	4.2	160.5	+5.4	4.8

Table 2. Comparison of Oil and Gas Production in the Caspian and Middle East, 2012.[21]

The ACG fields also produce a significant quantity of natural gas. In 2012, Azerbaijan's natural gas reserves were estimated at 0.9 Tcm and, like its oil, most of Azerbaijan's natural gas is produced from a few fields in the Caspian: ACG and Shah Deniz. Situated in the Caspian Sea around 60 miles southeast of Baku, the field's operator BP claims that Shah Deniz is one of the world's largest gas-condensate fields with over 1 Tcm of gas. Stage One of the field's development began operations in 2006, with an annual production capacity of 9 Billion cubic meters (Bcm).[22] Shah Deniz is significant because it is the only major field development in the Caspian Sea focused primarily on natural gas, rather than oil, despite the fact that, as mentioned earlier, the region is likely to be more gas- than oil-prone. With the exception of Shah Deniz, foreign investment in Azerbaijan's hydrocarbon sector (and across the Caspian) has centered on oil projects, which require less capital expenditure than natural gas projects, and less investment in infrastructure to get them started. Oil is also a more tradeable commodity than natural gas, which generally requires supply agreements to be in place before production begins.

Turkmenistan possesses some of the world's largest reserves of natural gas, as well as significant reserves of oil, although its ability to profit from these extensive hydrocarbon reserves has been restricted. In 2012 it had proven gas reserves of 17.5 Tcm, over 9 percent of total global reserves of natural gas, most of which is located onshore, in the east of the country; there is little in the Caspian Sea. While an independent audit of Turkmenistan's South Yolotan-Osman field in 2008 revealed huge quantities of natural gas, suggesting that the field may be one of the five largest in the world, in 2009 the Turkmen president dismissed the heads of several key gas departments for "falsification" of the data on natural gas reserves.[23] According to BP's *Statistical Review of World Energy*, in 2012 Turkmenistan had proven oil reserves of 0.6 billion barrels, the majority of which are located in the South Caspian Basin and onshore in the west of the country.[24] It also claims to have significant oil reserves in areas of the Caspian Sea that are subject to a dispute with Azerbaijan over ownership, notably the Serdar field (called Kyapaz by Azerbaijan), which lies on the maritime border between the two countries and has estimated recoverable reserves of 370-700 million barrels. Despite Turkmenistan seeking international arbitration to settle the boundary dispute, this issue, alongside Turkmenistan's claims to portions of the Azeri and Chirag fields (called Khazar and Osman by Turkmenistan) being developed by Azerbaijan, are still unresolved.

15

Russian production of oil and gas in the Caspian is limited: although it is thought that Russia may have estimated hydrocarbon reserves of up to 32 billion barrels of oil equivalent in its sector of the Caspian Sea, exploration has been limited to date. Between 1999 and 2005, the major Russian oil company, LUKoil, discovered six oil and gas fields in the northern sector of the Caspian, with total estimated reserves of 4.7 billion barrels. In 2010, the company began developing the Yury Korchagin offshore field, which holds an estimated 270 million barrels of oil and over 63 Bcm of natural gas.[25] It is important to note that the statistics in Table 1 for Russia include the whole of the country, not just its reserves in its sector of the Caspian Sea.

Potential hydrocarbon reserves in the Iranian sector of the Caspian remain largely unexplored, and there is no significant Iranian production in the Sea. According to the National Iranian Oil Company, the country's Sardar Jangal field in the Caspian contains significant reserves worth over U.S.$50 billion.[26] Iran announced at the end of 2011 that it had discovered the field, which it claims holds at least 1.4 Tcm of natural gas and as much as 100 million barrels of oil.[27] Despite these optimistic announcements, Iranian exploration and production in the Caspian is very limited, largely because its national sector of the Sea is very deepwater and therefore difficult to explore with its current technologies. U.S. and European sanctions have restricted the involvement of international oil majors in the country and, consequently, Iran's access to the most up-to-date production technologies. Furthermore, the Caspian Sea is not as important for Iran as it is for some of the other littoral states: Iran has reserves elsewhere that are much easier and cheaper to produce and transport to international markets. However, Iran is unlikely to commit to any common agreement on the Caspian Sea's legal status (discussed later) until it has fully explored its national sector, and thus, it will continue to be a spoiler in the Caspian region, blocking any prospective collective settlement.

Pipelines.

Azerbaijan, Kazakhstan, and Turkmenistan have considerable hydrocarbon reserves and hope to become major players on the world energy market. However, even if they increase the production of hydrocarbons, they still face several enduring obstacles: the difficulty of transporting products from the remote, landlocked Caspian region to lucrative international markets, together with the unclarified legal status of the Sea. Export infrastructure from the Caspian Sea region is still insufficient, and the development of additional export capacity is vital for future production growth. Limited export options, as well as reliance upon the Russian pipeline network and neighboring countries, have so far served to restrict the ability of the Caspian littoral countries to profit from their extensive oil and gas reserves. During the Soviet era, the routing of pipeline infrastructure was not a prominent issue for oil-producing areas of the USSR—pipelines were constructed to serve the needs of the Union, and thus, republics such as Azerbaijan and Kazakhstan were part of the national network, which generally flowed towards western Russia and Moscow. However, independence meant that the question of how to get oil and gas out of a relatively isolated area to international markets rose progressively to the top of the agenda for producers in the Caspian region. Until a decade ago, countries in the region were reliant

17

upon the Russian network of pipelines to reach European consumers, undermining their political and economic autonomy and giving Moscow substantial leverage. In 1997 Azeri President Heydar Aliyev announced that his country was "no longer prepared to be totally dependent upon Moscow" for the transit of its oil.[28] Consequently, there has been considerable investment in new international export pipelines over the past decade, which has led to the development of a southern oil and gas corridor between the Caspian and Mediterranean Seas and brought significant economic and security benefits. Pipelines have a permanency and an impact on political relations that highlight the strategic significance of hydrocarbons in the contemporary era. The static network of pipelines currently supplying Europe reflects the geopolitical situation of the Cold War, while new links demonstrate the geopolitical shift.

The focus to date has been on oil export infrastructure, symbolized by the ambitious Baku-Tbilisi-Ceyhan (BTC) project, a vital element in expanding oil production in the Caspian Basin.[29] The BTC (and BTE/ South Caucasus [SCP] gas) pipeline has considerable symbolic significance, providing a direct link between the Caspian region and Europe. Its construction has significantly altered the balance of power in the region, strengthening the political and economic autonomy of states such as Azerbaijan and Georgia, reducing Russian influence and cementing the involvement of Western actors such as Europe and the United States. Nevertheless, producers on the eastern side of the Caspian, Kazakhstan and Turkmenistan still remain largely reliant on the Russian pipeline network to get their hydrocarbons to Western markets.[30]

Kazakhstan has been seeking to keep its options open in terms of export routes. The Kazakhstan-China pipeline, which shipped its first oil in 2009, is a symbol of Beijing's strengthening ties with Central Asia (and China's first international oil pipeline), although all pipeline routes that run out of Kazakhstan toward the West cross Russian territory. Most Kazakh oil is exported via the Russian (and Chinese) pipeline network, including being shipped across the Caspian to terminals at Makhachkala and Taman and then on to the Russian Black Sea port of Novorossiisyk. Kazakhstan had been exporting Kazakh oil to international markets through the BTC, following a bilateral agreement with Azerbaijan in 2006. From 2008 to 2010, Kazakh oil transit via the BTC pipeline totaled 2.2 million tons, although Kazakhstan then switched to other export routes after disagreement over the conditions of shipment. It was reported at the end of 2013 that Kazakh oil would again be transported via the BTC: Tengizchevroil, the operator of the Tengiz field, announced it would be exporting 400,000 tons per month via the pipeline, shipping the oil across the Caspian by tanker.[31] The agreement also included provision for an increase in Kazakh oil shipments via the BTC to around 20 percent of the pipeline's throughput capacity by 2018-20, once production at the Kashagan field moves into its second phase. It is expected that Kazakhstan's oil exports will double once Kashagan is fully productive, necessitating a significant expansion of export infrastructure capacity, including greater use of the BTC and cross-Caspian tanker routes.

Kazakhstan has signed a memorandum with Azerbaijan on the development of a Kazakh Caspian Transportation System (KCTS), although progress has been slow. The agreement between KazMunaiGaz and SOCAR (the national oil companies of Kazakhstan and Azerbaijan), signed with the operators of the Kashagan and Tengiz fields, was intended to develop oil shipment routes to deliver crude from these two fields to the BTC and onward to international markets.[32] The KCTS is an integrated system consisting of a pipeline to transport crude from Eskene and Tengiz to an oil terminal in Kuryk on the Kazakh coast of the Caspian Sea, tankers and vessels to transport crude across the Caspian, an oil discharge terminal on the Azerbaijani coast, and connecting facilities to the BTC. The original agreement envisaged the project being operational by 2013-14, initially transporting up to 23 million tons of crude per year, increasing to 36 million tons. However, in 2010, KazMunaiGaz announced that implementation of the KCTS was being postponed because of delays on the Kashagan project, which is not expected to get underway until 2014 at the earliest.[33] Nevertheless, Kazakhstan still ships crude oil across the Caspian and exports it via Azerbaijan, as discussed previously. Azerbaijan's Energy Ministry expects around four million tons of Kazakh oil to be transported via Azeri territory in 2014.[34]

The three major littoral producers of oil and gas — Azerbaijan, Kazakhstan, and Turkmenistan — need to develop their maritime capabilities in order to be able to protect their interests in the Caspian Sea, including unexplored fields, production installations, and transport infrastructure such as tankers. Russia already dominates energy export infrastructure, giving it an undue amount of influence, and its investment in the Caspian Flotilla (whose roles include monitoring the extraction of hydrocarbons in disputed areas of the Sea) suggests a desire to maintain and possibly expand this influence. Some Russian observers have described the issue of pipelines in the landlocked Caspian region as a "battle for domination," particularly on the part of the United States, which "is seeking to accelerate the process of the political and economic isolation of former Soviet republics from Russia."[35] While this view ascribes little autonomy of action to the states involved, it does highlight the suspicion with which Moscow regards growing Western (particularly U.S.) influence in the Caspian region. Russian successes, such as the subsea Blue Stream gas pipeline, are considered to be the result of the "failure of American pipeline strategy in the Caucasus and Central Asia as a whole."[36] A major division has opened up between supporters of Russian and non-Russian export routes, which has the potential to produce new dividing lines in an already unstable region. In March 2008, Russian Foreign Minister Sergei Lavrov had scathing remarks about European plans for a Southern Corridor to transport energy from the Caspian region, describing the proposal for the multibillion-dollar, 3,900 kilometer (km) Nabucco pipeline linking Turkey and Austria as an "obviously artificial project." He stated that Russia has:

> answers that are economically more effective, and we are going to realise them. Blue Stream is already operational. The Caspian gas pipeline, expansion of the Central Asia-Centre gas pipeline, Burgas-Alexandroupolis, Nord Stream and South Stream: all these rest on a rational economic base.[37]

The decision to drop the Nabucco pipeline in favor of the more economically viable Trans-Adriatic (TAP)/Trans-Anatolian (TANAP) pipeline project suggests there was an element of truth in Lavrov's words. Nabucco was driven by political, rather than commercial, considerations, but the European Union (EU) appeared determined to drive it forward. The BTC was a triumph of politics over commercial sense; thus the precedent had been set. However, ultimately, shifts in the European gas market meant that Nabucco lost its strategic advantage, and the decision to abandon it was made on a commercial, not political, basis. The U.S.$7 billion, 2,000-km TANAP pipeline will initially transport up to 16 Bcm of gas (expected to reach 31 Bcm by 2023) from Azerbaijan to Turkey, where it will connect with the TAP, which links Turkey to Italy via Greece and Albania. The first gas flow is expected in 2018. These pipelines will be part of the Southern Gas Corridor, which will encompass planned infrastructure projects to transport natural gas from the Caspian and Middle East to European markets, in addition to existing supply corridors from Russia, Africa, and the North Sea. In its second *Strategic Energy Review*, released at the end of 2008, the European Commission (EC) called for the development of a Southern Gas Corridor to be recognized as an energy security priority for the EU, reducing European dependence on Russia as a supplier of oil and gas.[38]

The proposed Trans-Caspian Gas (TKG) Pipeline is a further element of the Southern Corridor, but, until recently, the project had been on the back burner. In 2011, Medvedev warned that construction of the pipeline, planned by Azerbaijan and Turkmenistan and supported by the EU, is unacceptable until all five littoral states have reached agreement over the legal status of the Sea, an issue that has remained unresolved since the collapse of the USSR. Nevertheless, Azerbaijan and Turkmenistan have declared that the TKG will cross the Caspian within their own national sectors and therefore the other littoral states have no say. In November 2013, the EU made it clear that it was intent on pushing ahead with the project, despite Russian unease. Denis Daniilidis, head of the EU mission in Turkmenistan, said that conditions were "most favourable" for the construction of the pipeline, and that the EU and Turkmenistan were in the final stages of their negotiations.[39] The 300-km pipeline will cross the Caspian from Turkmenistan to Azerbaijan, where it will feed into the South Caucasus country's existing gas export infrastructure. It will enable Turkmen gas to reach European consumers without having to transit through the Russian pipeline network. However, this will mean a reduction in transit tariffs for Moscow, which, as mentioned previously, is unhappy that the project may begin before final agreement between the Caspian Five on the Sea's legal status. Igor Bratchikov, the Russian president's special envoy for the delimitation and demarcation of borders with the Commonwealth of Independent States (CIS), warned of the potential "catastrophic" impact the pipeline could have on the Caspian's "extremely sensitive ecosystem," stating that in the event of an incident it would not be the Europeans (or Americans), but the littoral states who would have to tackle the aftermath.[40] While potential environmental damage is clearly a concern, Russia is using these instrumentally to mask its real concerns, namely, the loss of influence and transit tariffs that will result from the construction of the TKG. Mikhail Aleksandrov from Moscow's Institute of CIS countries has warned that "the West is underestimating Moscow's resolve to resort to force in order to prevent the realisation of pipeline projects across the Caspian Sea."[41] It is very unlikely that Moscow will resort to the use of force to prevent the construction of the TKG, although it is likely to continue to voice its opposition and use its influence to "persuade" Azerbaijan and Turkmenistan to abandon the project. Russia has watched its influence over pipelines and export infrastructure in the Caspian Basin erode over the past decade, which has had both an economic and political impact: Moscow has lost out on revenue from transit tariffs, but has also seen its political dominance undermined. The upgrade of the Caspian Flotilla is a strong signal that it is unwilling to cede any further influence and intends to remain the predominant power in the Caspian Sea region.

Cooperating for Caviar?

In addition to its significant hydrocarbon reserves, the Caspian contains another high-value natural resource: it is home to five of the most valuable species of sturgeon, which produce caviar. According to scientists from the Caspian Sea Fish Scientific-Research Institute, the commercial value of the Sea's biological wealth, if properly managed, amounts to 1.1 trillion rubles (U.S.$37 billion), equivalent to the total market value of the Sea's recoverable reserves of oil and gas.[42] This makes them highly sought after, by legal and illegal means, and illegal poaching of sturgeon is a serious problem for the littoral states. Poaching and uncontrolled fishing have had a dramatic impact on the Caspian's sturgeon population since the collapse of the Soviet Union: stocks of beluga sturgeon in the Sea have fallen by 30-40 percent over the past decade, and some species of the fish are on the verge of extinction.[43] According to the Iranian International Scientific Research Institute, at the current rate of decline, wild sturgeon may be extinct by 2021.[44]

Reflecting the lack of consensus about the Caspian's legal regime, the five littoral states have yet to reach agreement on the best way to manage the remaining sturgeon stocks. Russia introduced a ban on the commercial fishing of sturgeon in 2002 and a complete ban on all fishing in 2007, although there is an exemption for scientific research. The only legally available caviar in Russia currently comes from farmed (not wild) sturgeon. In 2012, head of Russia's Federal Fisheries Agency Andrei Krainy said that the ban on fishing may be lifted if the other four littoral states agreed to a 5-year moratorium to enable sturgeon stocks to recover.[45] Kazakhstan has banned sturgeon fishing in its sector of the Caspian. However, although the five littoral states formally agreed on an institutional mechanism and common environmental policy in the sea under the Framework Convention for Protection of the Marine Environment of the Caspian Sea signed in Tehran in 2006, the first legally binding regional agreement, they have yet to fully implement it or reach any common agreement on fishing quotas or a moratorium on fishing. Azerbaijan and Iran support a ban, but Turkmenistan does not.

As mentioned previously, poaching is a serious problem. Russia's Border Guards service said it seized seven tons of illegally caught sturgeon in 2011. In the first 10 days of a joint month-long operation conducted by Russian and Kazakh border guards in October 2013, over 17 km of net was seized, along with 10,000 fish hooks.[46] At the end of November 2013, Kazakh border guards killed a suspected Russian poacher during an anti-poaching operation in the Caspian. According to reports, eight small boats refused to stop for inspection, forcing the border guards to open fire.[47] The high value of the sturgeon and their caviar mean that poachers are willing to take greater risks to protect their income. According to one report, "80 percent of the poachers are now armed with small arms and grenades; the more sophisticated are even using space tracking systems to locate the exact position of the shoals," prompting Vladimir Putin to describe their activities as not just poaching, but "bioterrorism."[48] Given the high value of the sturgeon and the scale of illegal fishing and poaching, it is not surprising that the littoral states are investing in smaller, faster naval vessels in an attempt to interdict illegal activities and protect their national interests.

THE UNCLARIFIED LEGAL STATUS OF THE CASPIAN

The unclarified legal status of the Caspian Sea remains a serious impediment to the development of the region's natural resources (including sturgeon and hydrocarbon reserves) and the establishment of a stable security environment. It also facilitates illegal fishing and poaching. During the Soviet era, there were only two states bordering the Caspian Sea: the USSR and Iran. The collapse of the USSR in 1991 saw the appearance of four new states in its place — Azerbaijan, Kazakhstan, Russia, and Turkmenistan — all of whom had access to the Sea's valuable natural resources. The legal status of the Caspian Sea was thrown into doubt, and a dispute has been simmering since 1991. Ongoing negotiations between the Caspian Five have so far failed to establish whether the Caspian is legally considered to be a lake or inland sea. This lack of agreement means that the area remains one of political dispute that has, at times, threatened to turn into military action. In addition to the lack of clarity over the Sea's legal status and whether it is a sea or a lake, there is also disagreement among the littoral states over how to demarcate the Sea and what legal regime to apply (for example, median line or condominium).

Russia's position has shifted since 1991: Initially it supported the condominium approach, which would entail an equal division of the Sea among the five littoral states (giving them 20 percent each) and common sovereignty of its resources, without dividing it up into national zones. It was opposed to any unilateral action by the littoral states with regard to development of the Sea's resources and was furious when Azerbaijan announced its so-called "contract of the century" with international oil companies in 1994. However, by 1998, following the discovery of hydrocarbons in its sector of the Sea, the Russian government had moved to support a median-line approach, giving each state a share proportional to the length of its Caspian coastline. The year represented a turning point for the division of the Caspian. Viktor Kaluzhny, then Russia's Minister for Oil and Gas, stated that "[w]e will divide the seabed or, more precisely, the resources of the seabed. The water is common to all, it has no borders."[49] The lack of progress toward consensus among all five states stimulated bilateral negotiations between the three northern states. In 2002, Russia and Kazakhstan agreed to share the northern section of the Caspian seabed and established an official line demarcating the two national zones. Under the agreement, each country will exploit half of the three oil and gas fields in the disputed area, Kurmangazy, Tsentralnoye, and Khvalinskoye. In 2003, Russia, Azerbaijan, and Kazakhstan divided the northern 64 percent of the Caspian seabed into three unequal parts, using a median-line principle, giving Kazakhstan 27 percent; Russia, 19 percent; and Azerbaijan, 18 percent.

Iran believes that the status of the Caspian Sea should be resolved on the basis of consensus between the five littoral states and has rejected bi- and trilateral deals struck between Russia, Kazakhstan, and Azerbaijan. It supports the "condominium" concept and equal division of the Sea among the five littoral states. The Iranian government has also consistently insisted that the 1921 and 1940 agreements between the USSR and Tehran are to remain legally binding. This has put it in conflict with Azerbaijan, which is calling for the Law of the Sea (and thus a median-line principle) to be applied (under which Iran would get 14 percent) and has also continued to sign exploration agreements with oil companies despite the lack of consensus among the littoral states.

Iran wants a suspension of all oil and gas activity in disputed areas until an agreement has been reached on the division of the Caspian. Confrontation erupted in July 2001, when an Iranian warship threatened a geological survey ship in Azerbaijan's territorial waters. The ship was surveying the Alov-Sharg-Araz contract area (known as Alborz to the Iranians) for BP. The Iranian action was prompted by BP's plans to drill an exploration well at the Alov field in 2002 in the absence of a multilateral agreement on the Sea's legal status. The Azeri government claims that the disputed sector is located above the Astara-Gasankuli line, which links residential areas on the coasts of Azerbaijan and Turkmenistan. During the Soviet era, this line marked the Soviet-Iranian border in the Caspian Sea. BP subsequently suspended exploratory drilling at the site, scheduled for 2002. ExxonMobil also postponed the development of the offshore Savalan block, citing concerns about the unclarified legal status of the Caspian Sea. The 850-square-km block is located in the southern sector of the Caspian, an area that is the focus of a border dispute between Azerbaijan and Iran. These territorial disputes contribute to tensions between the two countries, which are exacerbated by Azerbaijan's burgeoning relationship with Israel (see Table 3).

Name	Who?
Azeri, Chirag (Khazar, Osman)	Azerbaijan Turkmenistan
Kyapaz (Serdar)	Azerbaijan Turkmenistan
Araz, Alov and Sharq (Alborz)	Azerbaijan Iran

Table 3. Fields Under Dispute.

Azerbaijan has also failed to resolve a dispute with Turkmenistan over ownership of specific fields in the Caspian, notably the Kyapaz field—called Serdar by Turkmenistan—which has estimated reserves of over 50 million tons. In May 2001, Turkmenistan threatened Azerbaijan with legal action after the failure of bilateral talks between the two countries on several disputed oil fields. The Azeri and Chirag fields, which are being developed by the AIOC as part of the "contract of the century," are also in dispute. Turkmenistan calls these fields Khazar and Osman and claims they lie partly in Turkmen territorial waters. Azerbaijan has offered to jointly develop the fields with Turkmenistan, but the latter has refused and, in 2009, Gurbanguly Berdymukhammedov announced that the government would seek dispute resolution at the International Court of Arbitration.[50]

Azerbaijan is the only littoral state to have formally asserted its sovereignty over its sector of the Caspian Sea in any official document. The country's constitution states that "[t]he internal waters of the Republic of Azerbaijan, the sector of the Caspian Sea (lake) belonging to the Republic of Azerbaijan, and the air space over the Republic . . . are integral parts" of the country's territory.[51] Despite the ongoing ownership disputes with Iran and Turkmenistan, the country has continued to develop its Caspian hydrocarbon resources and press ahead with negotiations on the proposed TKG highlighting Baku's belief that agreement on demarcation among all five states is not necessarily vital. In spite of Azerbaijan's confidence, the lack of consensus on the Sea's legal status impacts upon maritime navigation, environmental protection, pipeline construction, and exploitation of the Sea's natural resources, including its hydrocarbons and sturgeon.

THE CASPIAN AND RUSSIAN SECURITY

The Caspian Sea is part of Russia's "southern underbelly" (*yuzhnaya podbryush'ye*), a term that underscores the sense of vulnerability it feels along its southern border (which also includes the Caucasus). A 2009 article in the Russian military journal, *Voennaya Mysl'*, emphasized the significance of the "south," describing it as "the most worrying in terms of ensuring the national security of the Russian Federation. It is on our southern flank that events occur which directly affect national security and require a clear definition of Russia's geopolitical interests."[52] As discussed previously, the area is rich in resources, but also contains contested borders, increasing tension between states, notably Azerbaijan and Iran, and numerous transnational security challenges, including unresolved conflicts, organized crime, trafficking, and migration. Furthermore, it is an arena of competition between the principal regional and external powers. Thus, the Caspian is vital for Russian national security, both in terms of its natural resources and as a source of an array of cross-border security challenges, as evinced by the Caspian Flotilla's combat capability upgrade.

Russia's 2009 *National Security Strategy* (NSS) outlines the principal threats to Russian national security, including extremism, transnational criminal organizations, and illegal trafficking, noting that the protection of state borders was crucial to tackling these and preventing them from undermining Russian security. It identifies the Caspian region as an area from which particular challenges to Russian national interests and security may emanate and states that, in the future, there may be a competition for natural resources between states, which could lead to greater interest to traditionally Russian areas of interest:

> In the long term, the attention of international politics will be focused on ownership of energy resources, including in the Middle East . . ., the Arctic, in the Caspian basin and in Central Asia. . . . Under conditions of competition for resources, it is not excluded that arising problems may be resolved using military force, and that the current balance of power on the borders of Russia and its allies may be disturbed.[53]

The Caspian's hydrocarbon resources are unquestionably attracting considerable international interest and involvement, leading to a competition for influence between the major powers—demonstrated most recently by the sale of an 8.33 percent stake in the Kashagan development (held by major U.S. oil company ConocoPhillips) to China's CNPC, which was favored over India's ONGC. The growing presence of international actors in the Caspian region is of concern to Moscow, which perceives it to be a challenge to its own interests and influence in the area, especially with regard to pipelines. The NSS goes on to state that:

> The resolution of border security problems is achieved by creating high-technology and multifunctional border complexes, particularly on the borders with the Republic of Kazakhstan, Ukraine, Georgia and Azerbaijan, and likewise by increasing the effectiveness of state border defence, particularly in the Arctic zone of the Russian Federation, the Far East and on the Caspian.[54]

Russia's western coastline on the Caspian is a volatile neighborhood, containing the ongoing insurgency in the North Caucasus, which has engulfed Dagestan on the Caspian Sea. Although Moscow formally declared the end of its "counterterrorism operation" in Chechnya in the spring of 2009, it is still tackling an ongoing insurgency across the North Caucasus, and the region remains very unstable. In 2010, the Russian authorities admitted that the situation had deteriorated significantly, and that it is fighting an insurgency throughout the region. There has been a continuous campaign of assassinations targeted against local officials, particularly clerics and security representatives, and a string of terrorist attacks against economic targets such as railway lines, gas pipelines, and other strategic infrastructure. While the situation in Chechnya provided the inspiration for growing radicalism across the North Caucasus, recent violence in the region has been fueled by corrupt local governments, poverty, and the Kremlin's policy of seeking to exert direct control over republics; for example, appointing regional leaders instead of allowing them to be elected locally, as was previously the case. Dagestan, on the Caspian's western coast, has been particularly badly affected by the insurgency. This is of concern to the Caspian Flotilla, as the Kaspisyk base, where several of the most potent new ships are based (including the Gepard class *Dagestan* and *Tatarstan*), is located only 20 km from the Dagestani capital, Makhachkala.

Interestingly, when Russian Defense Minister Sergei Shoigu identified three principal military threats to Russian security in November 2013, the North Caucasus insurgency was not on the list, although international Islamist terrorism was. In addition to this, he specified the withdrawal of Western coalition forces from Afghanistan in 2014 and continued NATO enlargement on Russia's borders.[55] The Russian government is very concerned about the impact of ISAF's withdrawal from Afghanistan in 2014 and the potential for instability affecting its Central Asian neighbors and, ultimately, Russia. Konstantin Sokolov, vice president of Russia's Academy of Geopolitical Problems, highlighted Russian concerns about instability in the wider Middle East region spreading to Russia and the Caspian region:

> What happens in the Near East reaches Russia fairly quickly. The conflict will move in the direction of Iran, and this is already the Caspian region. If combat operations begin in Iran, the strategic ties between that country and China, which receives energy sources from Iran, will be disturbed. There is a danger of the undermining of stability in Central Asia. It would not be difficult to do this, because the economic situation of the majority of inhabitants there is very difficult. From there, the conflict would cross into Russia.[56]

The upgrade of the Caspian Flotilla highlights the sense of vulnerability Russia feels along its southern periphery. Stability and predictability are core concerns for Russia in the Caspian region, and Russia is seeking to assert its control over the area to ensure these objectives, which potentially could be undermined by security challenges such as the activity of terrorist and extremist groups and criminal organizations, as well as the increasing influence of external actors, particularly the United States and the West. Russia is keen to reassert its influence, both within the Caspian region and across the former Soviet space, to counter the perceived expansion of Western involvement, within its "sphere of influence." The decision to upgrade the Caspian Flotilla was made over a decade ago, at a time of growing concern about rising Western interest in the region. On his arrival in the Kremlin in 2000, Putin was determined to reassert Russian influence in the Caspian region to counter the growing influence of external actors such as Turkey, the United Kingdom (UK) and the United States. The issue was considered of such importance that it was discussed at a session of the Russian Security Council in April 2000. Putin was quoted in Russian media reports as stating:

> We must understand that the interest of our partners in other countries—Turkey, Great Britain, and the USA—toward the Caspian Sea is not accidental. This is because we are not active. We must not turn the Caspian Sea into yet another area of confrontation, no way. We just have to understand that nothing will fall into our lap out of the blue, like manna from heaven. This is a matter of competition and we must be competitive.[57]

Putin's statement reflects the broader Russian political narrative, which remains dominated by talk of "competition" and the need to be "competitive" with the West, highlighting the zero-sum approach that Moscow tends to take in its foreign policy: the statement above suggests there is little room for cooperation or collaboration. Russia's response to suggestions that the United States may establish a presence at the Kazakh port of Aqtau, as a means of getting its military equipment out of Afghanistan, highlighted its opposition to the presence of any external actors in the closed system of the Caspian Sea, as mentioned earlier. Russian sentiments reflect those of the other littoral states: the leaders of the Caspian Five have long made it clear that the presence of external forces in the Sea would not be tolerated. This was noted in a formal document for the first time in the declaration signed by the Caspian Five at the Second Summit Meeting of Caspian Heads of State held in 2007 in Tehran, in which the littoral states formally agreed to deny access to third states who wished to use the region to launch military operations against any Caspian state, in an attempt to promote stability across the region. The declaration also stated that only littoral states were permitted to deploy ships and military forces in the Sea, again seeking to limit the influence of external actors, particularly the United States and the North Atlantic Treaty Organization (NATO). Regional stability is particularly important for Caspian states, as instability or renewed conflict could have a negative impact on the development of their hydrocarbon potential, including the construction of new export infrastructure, and deter vital foreign investment, ultimately undermining their economic development and possible internal political stability.

It has been suggested that an important objective of Russian foreign policy is the establishment of a multipolar world, an aim that can be achieved by securing the country's geopolitical interests in various "vectors" encompassing the "southern geopolitical vector," which includes the Caspian region and the Caucasus.[58] This is reflected in key Russian strategic documents, including the 2008 *Foreign Policy Concept*, 2009 *National Security Strategy* and 2010 *Military Doctrine*. All three documents emphasize the importance of a multipolar world, reflecting Moscow's unhappiness with U.S. dominance of the international system, which it feels is destabilizing. The Kremlin has become increasingly concerned about growing U.S. (and European) influence in areas traditionally perceived as Russia's "strategic backyard," that is, in former Soviet states such as Georgia, Ukraine, and the Central Asian republics. In an attempt to counterbalance Western influence in the post-Soviet space and retain its leverage, the Kremlin is seeking to reassert its influence by political, economic, and military means. The military aspect of this approach is vital, as it provides credibility to the potential to project influence: without an effective and visible military capability, Russia's ability to influence events in the Caspian would be undermined. Thus, the efficacy of Russian efforts to preserve its influence has been underpinned by its considerable military footprint across the "south."

THE CASPIAN FLOTILLA

The Caspian is central to the maintenance of Russian national security, both in terms of its natural resources and as a source of an array of cross-border security challenges, demonstrated by the Caspian

Flotilla's combat capability upgrade. The Russian Ministry of Defence describes the Caspian Flotilla as "the guarantor of the integrity of maritime boundaries and the most important foreign policy tool of the state in the Caspian Sea,"[59] highlighting the significance of the Flotilla for contemporary Russian security and the reason it is one of Russia's only naval forces that has seen a growth in strength, rather than a reduction, in recent years, under Putin's leadership.

Following the disintegration of the USSR in 1991, the Soviet Caspian Flotilla was divided evenly between the four former Soviet littoral states on the Caspian: Azerbaijan, Kazakhstan, Russia, and Turkmenistan. Kazakhstan and Turkmenistan ceded their share to Moscow, which operated a joint flotilla under Russian command.[60] This joint flotilla was transitory, however, and the newly independent states soon decided to establish their own independent naval capabilities. The Flotilla's base moved from Baku (now in independent Azerbaijan) to Astrakhan, a Russian port city at the mouth of the Volga River. It is estimated that Russia's Caspian Flotilla initially comprised only of two frigates, approximately 12 patrol boats and some smaller vessels, and there was little investment in new equipment. This changed with Putin's arrival in the Kremlin in 2000. One of his first priorities on taking power was to halt the perceived decline of the Russian armed forces. A program of reform was launched to modernize the armed forces, making them smaller, more affordable, and more flexible, configured to fight small, low-intensity regional conflicts as well as high-intensity global war. Military reform has led to cuts in both personnel and equipment, with the aim of creating a more mobile military with an expeditionary focus. The Pacific Fleet was slated to lose 5,000 personnel, while overall the Navy's inventory was expected to be slashed from 240 vessels to 123 by 2016.[61]

However, there has also been considerable investment in modernization and rearmament. In September 2010, Russian Defense Minister Anatoly Serdyukov declared that annual defense spending for the period 2010-20 was expected to equate to 3.8 percent of the gross domestic product.[62] In 2011, Dmitry Medvedev announced that over U.S.$700 billion would be allocated to modernize Russia's defense armaments over the period 2011-20, although it was revealed in August 2012 that as much as 70 percent of this would be held until after 2016.[63] Thus, the modernization of the Caspian Flotilla is part of a wider expansion and renewal of Russia's naval (and broader military) capabilities. The Flotilla has recovered from the collapse of the USSR in 1991 (and the subsequent redeployment from Baku to Astrakhan) and has been the focus of significant investment in recent years: by 2020, the Caspian Flotilla will have received as many as 16 new vessels, a striking amount for a relatively minor fleet operating in a closed basin (see Table 4). In addition to new vessels, the Flotilla has also acquired a new base at Kaspisysk, following a decision by the Russian naval command in 2010 to concentrate its missile grouping there. While Astrakhan is still Russia's principal port on the Caspian, it has invested in the development of this new port in the volatile North Caucasus republic of Dagestan.

Name	Class	Type	Year Commissioned
Dagestan	Gepard	Frigate	2012
Tatarstan	Gepard	Frigate	2003
Makhachkala	Buyan	Corvette	2012
Volgodonsk	Buyan	Corvette	2011
Astrakhan	Buyan	Corvette	2006
Grad Sviyazhsk	Buyan-M	Corvette	2013
Uglich	Buyan-M	Corvette	2013
Veliky Ustyug	Buyan-M	Corvette	under construction
Zelyony Dol	Buyan-M	Corvette	under construction
Serpukhov	Buyan-M	Corvette	under construction
Borovsk	Matka	Hydrofoil missile boat	1983
Buddenovsk	Matka	Hydrofoil missile boat	1983
various	Serna	Landing craft	5 in service; 3 purchased in 2013

Table 4. Caspian Flotilla Vessels.

Russia is focused on the establishment of forces that are able to deploy rapidly and cope with instability on its periphery, but that also signals its intent to remain a dominant force in the region. Speaking in 2012 prior to the commissioning of the *Dagestan Gepard* class frigate, Dagestani president Magomedsalam Magomedov voiced his pleasure that "one of Russia's most powerful ships" was to be based on the Caspian:

> It is good news for our foreign allies, and a weighty argument for those who are not. Today, the Caspian Sea and Caucasus are places where interests of various powers intersect, so Russia must have a mighty fleet here. I'm sure that the frigate *Dagestan* and further ships will strengthen that might.[64]

The *Dagestan* is armed with the Kalibr-NK system, making it far more potent than her sister ship, the *Tatarstan*, both of which are located in Kaspisyk. According to the Russian Ministry of Defense, the frigate, which is "absolutely invisible to enemy radar," is armed with cruise missiles that have a range of over 2,000 km and "considerably boost Russia's military capability. . . . [N]o other flotilla on the Caspian has systems effective against both ships and land targets":

> The *Dagestan* in effect heralds the start of qualitative and comprehensive re-equipment of the Caspian Flotilla as a whole, moreover, not just technically, but also conceptually. As early as next year [2013], the Russian Navy on the Caspian will add at least three more mobile, quick ships armed with cruise missiles. This type of armament at sea is now becoming the main one. By 2015, the Flotilla will be renewed almost completely.[65]

The *Dagestan* frigate is just one of a range of new vessels that have been commissioned into the Caspian Flotilla over the past decade (see Table 4), developed to operate in shallow littoral waters, rather than blue-water operations. The *Makhachkala*, *Volgodonsk*, and *Astrakhan* are the Caspian Flotilla's small artillery ships. These *Buyan* class littoral patrol vessels cost an estimated U.S.$20 million each and are relatively heavily armed for their size, equipped with SA-16 Gubka (Strelets) surface-to-air missiles and a rapid-firing main gun with a 15-km range. Each ship also has two 30 milimeter (mm) six-barreled AK-630 cannons, two 14.5-mm machine guns, three 7.62-mm machine guns and a UMS-73 Grad-M 122-mm multiple rocket launcher.[66] The *Buyan-M* variant is a more heavily armed version. The *Grad Sviyazhsk* is the lead ship of the Caspian Flotilla's *Buyan-M* class small guided-missile ship series, which also includes the *Uglich*, *Velikiy Ustyug*, and the *Zelenyy Dol* (currently under construction in Tatarstan). They are multi-purpose river/sea ships equipped with the Kalibr-NK anti-ship missile system, 100-mm and 30-mm guns, as well as Igla-1M air defense missiles.[67] They also incorporate "stealth" technology for a reduced radar signature: inclined flat superstructure surfaces, hull skirting, doors, and hatches concealed within the superstructure and deck.[68] According to the Ministry of Defense, the *Buyan-M* class ships are intended to protect Russia's offshore economic zones and have been designed to engage surface warships in littoral areas and rivers.[69] This reflects the roles assigned to the Caspian Flotilla, which includes the protection of Russian shipping, as well as providing protection to Russian hydrocarbon production facilities at sea against potential threats, monitoring the extraction of hydrocarbons and bio-resources in disputed areas of the Sea.

In addition to the new vessels, the strike power of the Flotilla has also been augmented by a separate coastal missile battalion that was established at the beginning of 2011, equipped with Bal-E anti-ship missiles with a range of 130 km. Speaking in November 2012, commander of the Caspian Flotilla Rear-Admiral Sergei Alekminskiy discussed the modernization of the Caspian Flotilla, outlining the Podsolnykh over-the-horizon radar station for aerial and surface observation and the new coastal battalion:

> We set up last year, and are making operational this year, a permanent–readiness shore battery equipped with the latest Bal missile, which has already been fired. . . . By 2016 the Caspian Flotilla will have a solid missile and gunnery group.[70]

The Bal coastal missile complex is capable of engaging targets up to 120 km away and includes a self-propelled command, control, and communications post, as well as a self-propelled launcher and other vehicles.[71] It has a defensive posture, which raises questions about the threat Russia sees approaching its territory from the waters of the Caspian. The acquisition of the system by the Caspian Flotilla also highlights Russia's sense of vulnerability in the region and the desire to secure itself against all possible threats, both traditional state-based threats and nontraditional transnational security challenges such as trafficking and extremism. The Russian Navy has also purchased three additional *Serna* class landing craft for the Caspian Flotilla in addition to those already in service. The landing craft are air-cushioned, enabling them to deploy troops onshore more easily than ordinary vessels, and can carry either one tank or two infantry fighting vehicles, or a 92-man landing party.[72]

The new vessels have been put through their paces in several national and international exercises in the Caspian Sea. The Caspian Flotilla took part in Russia's annual Kavkaz-2012 exercises, practicing "measures for maintaining favourable operational conditions in formations, areas of responsibility, defending the basing area and areas of economic activity, and blockading the coast."[73] Over 500 troops were put through a "mock offensive" operation, and there was a joint missile firing session that included a strike force of ships (including the *Tatarstan, Dagestan, Borovsk*, and *Budennovsk*) and the BAL coastal defense missile system, firing anti-ship cruise missiles at the "enemy's" force of amphibious warfare ships.[74] A squad of divers operating from the *Astrakhan* in the northern Caspian also fired underwater arms and hand-held grenade launchers at a sailing object, according to the Interfax-AVN military news agency. Furthermore, a group of trawlers destroyed mines "using their artillery systems."[75] Speaking at the opening of the Kavkaz-2012 exercises, Putin stated that the exercises had one objective: "[T]he Armed Forces must demonstrate their readiness to defend our national interest and show that they are ready to decisively rebuff any threats or challenges to Russia's national security."[76]

The Flotilla held another series of exercises in August 2013, including missile launches, artillery fire, a simulated sea battle, and minesweeping. A total of 10 warships and support vessels took part, along with over 1,300 servicemen and a BAL coastal missile system. According to the Russian Ministry of Defense the BAL missile complex performed a combat exercise involving the detection and launch of a missile strike on an adversary's flotilla.[77] Interestingly, the exercise involved rehearsing maneuvers against an opposing group of combat vessels, as well as thwarting plans to land an assault force, all moves that anticipate offensive action from a state, rather than nonstate, actor: nonstate actors such as transnational extremist groups are unlikely to deploy a detachment of combat vessels or to be able to marshal the numbers necessary to land an assault force. This raises questions as to the perceived threat that the Russians are preparing to counter. The August 2013 exercises appear to be intended to simulate offensive action by a state, but, as the Caspian Sea is a closed body of water, this leads to the conclusion that the state on the attack would be a littoral state. Furthermore, Russian policy documents such as the NSS and *Military Doctrine* indicate that, with the exception of NATO enlargement, the greatest national security challenges come from nonstate actors such as criminals, smugglers, and extremists.

Little wonder that in an article published in 2011, Mikhail Barabanov dismissed the Caspian Flotilla, stating that its existence did not "make any practical sense because of the weakness of the naval forces of the other Caspian states and the absence of any real missions with respect to the combat use of the flotilla."[78] Questions over the Flotilla's combat role were also highlighted during Tsentr-2011, an exercise held for member-states of the Collective Security Treaty Organization (CSTO) that included a joint exercise that involved Russia's Caspian Flotilla, the Kazakh Navy, and the air forces of both countries repelling a theoretical attack against Kazakhstan—the objective of which was to seize oil fields. According to an analysis of the exercise in *Nezavisimaya Gazeta*, the Russo-Kazakh grouping "repelled massive enemy missile strikes, the landing of a hostile amphibious assault force and a ground invasion by . . . mechanised columns."[79] However, the analysis raised questions about the perceived enemy:

> From where in a closed sea-lake, the only exit from which is completely controlled by Russia, will you get enemy ship groupings, capable of landing assault forces and supporting them with fire from the sea? And in the process this mysterious enemy will also inflict massive air strikes and will carry out a ground invasion! What country is this? Is it really Iran? There simply aren't any other candidates, as the ships of non-littoral states cannot enter the Caspian Sea without Russian authorisation. But the Iranian Navy is totally incapable of conducting these operations on the Caspian.[80]

OTHER CASPIAN NAVIES

Russia's investment in its Caspian Flotilla has been reflected by an increase in expenditure and capabilities of the other four littoral states. After years of under-funding, Azerbaijan, Kazakhstan, and Turkmenistan have been upgrading their naval capabilities recently, largely to ensure better control over their oil and gas reserves and installations in the Caspian.

Kazakhstan.

Although it withdrew from the joint flotilla under Russian command in 1994, it was not until 2003, more than 10 years after independence, that Kazakhstan established its own naval forces. The decision followed the discovery of the giant Kashagan offshore oilfield and the realization that an effective naval force was required, if only to protect the country's hydrocarbon installations and resources. Its 2011 *Military Doctrine* identified the need to upgrade "military and other infrastructure" in the Caspian region, noting that the "unresolved legal status of the Caspian Sea, the effort of some Caspian countries to increase their military capability, and the disputed oilfields could worsen the regional military-political situation."[81] According to Commander in Chief of the Navy Rear Admiral Zhandarbek Zhanzakov, the upgrading of the Caspian Flotilla is also a factor in the development of a Kazakh navy:

> [A]nalysis of the naval forces of our neighbours shows their rapid development in order to change the current state of affairs in their favour. For example, two frigates—*Tatarstan* and *Dagestan*—equipped with modern missile systems and the new generation. . . . *Astrakhan*, built using stealth technology. . . .[82]

In 2012, Kazakhstan launched its first domestically built *Katran* class missile patrol ship, the *Kazakhstan*, equipped with "modernised anti-aircraft missile and artillery units." The ship is the first of three to be built at the Zenit shipyards in Uralsk, Kazakhstan.[83] According to a 2012 report in *Jane's Navy International*, Kazakhstan also intends to procure three corvettes, possibly from South Korea,[84] and there were also reports that it was considering the MBDA MM40 Exocet Block 3 anti-ship missile as a coastal defense weapon.[85] Nevertheless, despite these plans and the modernization of port infrastructure at Aqtau, Kuryk, and Bautino, Kazakhstan has one of the weakest naval forces in the Caspian region, and the country needs to develop its naval forces to be able to protect its interests in the Caspian Sea and provide security for its offshore oil and gas installations, particularly Kashagan. As noted earlier, the Kazakh sector of the Caspian Sea is much shallower and thus impacts upon security: the offshore Kashagan field is potentially vulnerable, since it is located in shallow waters that freeze in winter, facilitating access by poachers, for example.

Azerbaijan.

Like Kazakhstan, Azerbaijan's defense priorities in the Caspian Sea are to protect its coastline and guard oil and gas installations. Despite significant spending on defense (reported to be over U.S.$3 billion in 2013), Azerbaijan has prioritized spending on its land and air forces, rather than its navy, because of the unresolved dispute with Armenia over Nagorno-Karabakh. There has been some investment in naval capabilities, and Azerbaijan intends to boost its capacities in the Caspian as part of a naval modernization program. A new base for the country's naval forces is under construction at Puta (in Baku's Garabagh district), to replace the historic base in Baku, which should be operational by 2014, and the country also has plans to commence indigenous production of warships, although few details of this have been released.[86]

The U.S. Caspian Guard initiative has strengthened the naval capabilities of both Azerbaijan and Kazakhstan, providing training and equipment to the two countries in an attempt to help address counterproliferation, counterterrorism, and illicit trafficking as well as the protection of key economic zones, particularly hydrocarbon installations. Launched in 2003, the Caspian Guard has assisted the two countries in the integration of their airspace and maritime surveillance and control systems; their national command, control, communications, computers, and intelligence systems; and their reaction and response forces.[87] American aid was forthcoming to assist Azerbaijan's State Border Service in installing engineering equipment on the country's southern borders in order to boost security, and the service was presented with U.S. cutters. Joint U.S.-Azeri naval exercises have been held in the Caspian Sea, highlighting the strategic importance of the region to the United States.[88] The exercise angered Iran, which accused Baku of breaching an agreement between the Caspian Five that other countries not become involved in the settlement of regional problems.[89]

The United States has supplied Azerbaijan's naval vessels with radar and communication equipment to help improve command and control.[90] These initiatives have facilitated the development of new capabilities aimed at countering terrorism as well as smuggling, narcotics trafficking, and organized crime on the

Caspian Sea. Furthermore, as part of the Weapons of Mass Destruction Proliferation Prevention Program, Azerbaijan's coastal security has been strengthened by the use of a series of coastal radar stations, which, according to the U.S. State Department, is used "by the Navy, Coast Guard, and State Border Service to conduct maritime surveillance and detect smuggling threats."[91] However, these capability enhancements have focused on "softer" security challenges and, according to one assessment, have "not given Azerbaijan any offensive capabilities beyond an enhanced command and control and radar-based surface monitoring system, thereby depriving Azerbaijan of . . . the ability for real power projection."[92] This could be changed if the country begins to develop its own naval warships. According to a report on the website of Turkish newspaper *Today's Zaman* in October 2012, Azerbaijan has ordered anti-ship missiles from Israel. The article analyzed this order in the context of poor relations between Baku and Tehran, and Iran's "aggressive" behavior with regard to the Caspian Sea.[93] Continuing tension between Azerbaijan and Iran has been exacerbated by Baku's burgeoning relationship with Israel. Israel is reportedly providing Azerbaijan with Gabriel-5 anti-ship missiles, possibly to counter any potential threat from Iran. The growing number of Iranian naval vessels in the Caspian would enable Iran to support its territorial claims in the Sea and bring it into conflict with Azerbaijan.

Turkmenistan.

Like those of Kazakhstan and Azerbaijan, Turkmenistan's navy is also undergoing expansion after years of underfunding, as the government seeks to ensure it is able to control and protect its hydrocarbon resources in the Caspian amid its ownership dispute with Azerbaijan. Until recently, Turkmenistan was considered to have the weakest navy among the Caspian littoral states: long regarded as constituting little more than a coastguard service, the navy has been upgrading both its infrastructure and fleet to improve its capabilities. The United States has provided Turkmenistan with a patrol boat, *Point Jackson*, to boost maritime security on the Caspian Sea, and, in 2009, Turkmenistan procured two Russian-built patrol boats with speeds of up to 50 knots.[94] Two years later, it acquired two Russian-built *Molniya* class Project 12418 corvettes, armed with 16 Uran-E missile systems each, and reportedly has plans for procuring three more in the near future.[95] Turkmenistan also ordered two 57m NTPB (new Type Patrol Boat) vessels from the Dearsan Shipyard in Turkey in 2010. According to a report in 2011, the Turkmen navy and coastguard constituted around 2,000 personnel and 16 vessels, up from less than 1,000 in 2006.[96] The new vessels are equipped with surface-to-surface missiles, several guns, and short-range Igla manportable missiles. In addition to the purchase of new vessels, in 2009 President Berdymukhamedov announced plans to establish a naval base on the country's southern Caspian coastline.[97] The base is intended to facilitate the protection of maritime borders and protect the state from external threats such as smuggling and terrorism. The Turkmen president made it clear that the navy would not be used to settle territorial disputes with its neighbors, warning that there are "international terrorist groups" who would "like to disturb the Turkmen people's peaceful life."[98] Berdymukhamedov has said that the establishment of the Turkmen navy should be completed by 2015, but has not specified how large it will be. Although these acquisitions have significantly improved Turkmenistan's naval capabilities in the Caspian Sea, it remains one of the weaker naval forces in the region.

Iran.

Under the terms of the Russian-Persian agreements of the 19th century (the 1813 Treaty of Gulestan and the 1828 Treaty of Turkmenchai), Iran was not permitted to develop its naval forces in the Caspian Sea. This ban was maintained in the Soviet-Iranian treaties of 1921 and 1940, so it was not until the 1990s that Iran was able to focus on the development of a Caspian fleet. Over the past decade, Iran has sought to make up for lost time and has begun to build up its naval capabilities in the Caspian. The naval base at the commercial port of Bandar-Anzali has been developed, while the infrastructure at other Caspian ports such as Nowshahr and Babolsar is reported to have undergone modernization.[99] In 2004, Tehran launched a *Sina* class fast attack craft, launching another two in 2006 and 2009,[100] and in March 2013, it announced the launch of the *Jamaran-2 Mowdge* class frigate (the *Velayat*) into the Caspian Sea at the port of Bandar-Anzali. Iranian officials described the indigenously manufactured *Jamaran-2* as a message of "peace and friendship," although, inaugurating the vessel, President Mahmoud Ahmadinejad undermined this message by describing the ship as a "destroyer there to meet those who want to jeopardise the security of surrounding nations."[101]

According to Iran's Press-TV, production of the *Jamaran-2* frigate began 2 years ago specifically with the "aim of protecting Iran's 20 percent share of the Caspian Sea."[102] This statement highlights Iran's determination to increase its territorial claim in the Caspian, from the 14 percent accorded it under international law to the 20 percent it believes it is actually due. The launch of the frigate heightened concerns about Iranian intentions to support its territorial claims in the Caspian. At 94 meters long, the frigate is the second largest warship in the Caspian after Russia's two *Gepard* class frigates, the *Dagestan* and *Tatarstan*. Harmer believes the frigate's launch was intended to "underscore the extent of Iranian commitment to protecting and possibly expanding its interests in the Caspian" and reinforced a 2012 minelaying and minesweeping exercise held in Iran's sector of the Sea, which "was . . . part of a broader Iranian effort to secure its territorial claims in the Caspian."[103] He goes on to argue that, whatever its intentions may be, "it is a sign of Iranian resiliency and depth of industrial capacity that the Islamic Republic is able to conduct significant exercises and launch indigenously produced ships along multiple fronts."[104]

The launch of the *Jamaran-2* followed an Iranian threat in June 2012 to deploy *Ghadir* class midget submarines in the Caspian against a backdrop of worsening relations with Baku over the latter's blossoming relationship with Israel. One analyst suggested the threatened deployment and expanded naval capabilities in the Caspian could enable Iran to deter any further cooperation between Azerbaijan and Israel.[105] Certainly, Iran's capabilities in the Caspian Sea are no longer solely defensive: they have acquired offensive capabilities.

Iran's development of its naval capabilities in the Caspian is an important factor in the reshaping of Russian-Iranian relations, which could see the two states expanding their political cooperation into more active military cooperation. Putin has made mention in the past of forming some kind of alliance with Tehran, but this has been undermined by the fact that both states have very different expectations of their relationship. Nevertheless, they do share a common desire to limit the influence of external actors in the Caspian region, particularly the United States. Russia and Iran are seeking to strengthen their bilateral relationship, including naval cooperation, to boost maritime security in the Caspian Sea and ensure that their influence is not eroded by the appearance of actors from outside of the region. Speaking in November 2012, commander of the Caspian Flotilla Rear-Admiral Sergei Alekminskiy suggested that ships from the Caspian Flotilla could pay their first visit in 40 years to an Iranian port during 2013, stating that the Minister of Foreign Affairs would decide whether such a visit should go ahead, but that "we wish to see how the Iranian fleet is progressing."[106] This wish was partially fulfilled when two Iranian vessels docked in Astrakhan for 4 days in June 2013, the first time Iranian naval ships had been to Russia. According to Iran's defense attaché in Moscow Colonel Soleiman Adeli, the Iranian-built ships were intended to "consolidate maritime relations between Tehran and Moscow, and promote peace and friendship" among the five littoral states:

> Iran and Russia both want Caspian Sea littoral states to maintain the security of the body of water without any interference from extra-regional powers. They regard the presence of outsiders in the sea as a source of tension and division.[107]

The two countries appear to be seeking to use their expanding naval capabilities to maintain the status quo in the Caspian Sea region, which is to their own advantage, and deter other littoral states from developing effective relationships with external actors. This undermines the sovereignty of those states and their ability to pursue an autonomous foreign policy. It also has significant implications for states outside the region, such as the United States, who wish to deepen their engagement with, and influence on, the Caspian states. If Moscow and Tehran can get over their mutual suspicions and rivalry, they could be a powerful international force. Their relationship is driven by economic pragmatism and self-interest: Iran is a key economic partner for Russia, one of its largest customers for conventional weapons, as well as nuclear energy. Russia has also been one of Iran's biggest supports in the United Nations, blocking sanctions and resolutions that would damage Iran and its ally, Syria. However, although Moscow is a strong supporter of Iran's right to develop a peaceful nuclear program, it is wary of Tehran's nuclear aspirations and certainly does not want to encourage the development of a nuclear power on its southern periphery.

COMPETING OR COOPERATING?

Russia is clearly wary of Iranian motives in the Caspian, but it is also keen to prevent any external actor gaining a foothold in the region, which is very unlikely given the closed nature of the Sea. Table 5 illustrates Russian naval dominance in the region. Although there are no figures for Iran's naval presence on the Caspian Sea, the fact that it has only recently started to develop its naval capabilities in the region suggests the number of Iranian vessels on the Caspian is minimal and currently poses little challenge to Russia. However, Iran is in the process of developing its naval forces in the Caspian, which may, in the future, threaten Moscow's dominance. In his State of the Nation speech in December 2013, Putin affirmed that Russia will not allow any country to achieve military superiority over it, stating that:

> no one should entertain any illusions about achieving military superiority over Russia; we will never allow it. Russia will respond to all these challenges, both political and technological. We have all we need in order to do so.[108]

	Population (million)	Armed Forces	Navy
Azerbaijan	9.49	66,950	2,200
Iran	78.86	523,000	In Caspian?
Kazakhstan	17.52	39,000	3,000
Turkmenistan	5.05	22,000	500
Russia	142.86	845,000	20,000 (Caspian Flotilla)

Table 5. Caspian Naval Forces.

The developments outlined in Table 5 suggest that the Caspian Sea is becoming increasingly militarized and raise the specter of a potential arms race in the region: where Russia leads, the other four littoral states are bound to follow. If Moscow is arming itself to defend against an array of perceived security challenges, then logically the other Caspian states are bound to be impacted by this. However, the littoral states are aware of the potential escalation that ongoing militarization may bring. In 1992, Iran stressed that the Caspian was a "sea of peace and friendship," calling for it to remain "nonmilitary."[109] The theme of peace and cooperation has been continued, and Azerbaijan's President Ilham Aliyev has stated:

> Azerbaijan has always favoured demilitarisation of the Caspian. Although we have a navy to help us protect our interests, we believe that the Caspian should be demilitarised, it must become a zone of peace. Cooperation, not rivalry, should prevail.[110]

Speaking at the 34th meeting of the Working Group on the Convention on the legal status of the Caspian Sea held in Moscow in November 2013, Russian Foreign Minister Sergei Lavrov stressed that under contemporary conditions, "it is crucially important to keep the Caspian region as a zone of peace, friendship and good neighbourliness."[111] He went on to say that Russia will continue using existing mechanisms to address "all fundamental Caspian issues only among 'the five' whose members have exclusive sovereign rights over the sea and its resources," again highlighting Russia's opposition to external actors playing any role in the negotiations.[112] In his view, interference by external actors in Caspian issues does not help in their resolution. In an attempt to counter what it perceived to be a growing U.S. influence in the Caspian region (evidenced by Caspian Guard and the growing presence of international energy companies), in 2005 Lavrov proposed the creation of a common regional security alliance to include all five littoral states, the Caspian Naval Group for Operational Cooperation (KASFOR). The initiative was designed to counter common security challenges such as terrorism and potential military threats. However, the proposal failed to gain the support of all littoral states, some of whom were wary of joining a Russian-dominated security structure: although Iran was one of the first states to voice its support for the grouping, Azerbaijan refused to join, while Turkmenistan's declared policy of neutrality in international affairs precluded its participation. KASFOR remains on the drawing board, and there is no single regional security system that includes all five Caspian states. In 2006, Russia proposed the establishment of a regional rapid reaction force in the Caspian Sea to tackle terrorism and other security challenges, another proposal that failed to get off the ground.[113]

There have been several other feeble attempts by the Caspian Five to establish multilateral cooperation on issues of regional security, with varying degrees of success. The first Summit Meeting of Caspian Heads of State took place in Turkmenistan in 2002. Despite agreeing to meet on an annual basis thereafter, the second meeting took place 5 years later in Tehran. At that meeting, the Caspian Five leaders adopted a 25-point declaration that pledged to seek to build and enhance mutual confidence, regional security, and stability, calling for:

> peaceful, just, and stable solutions to conflicts in line with the United Nations charter, also taking into account sovereignty, territorial integrity and the inviolability of internationally recognized borders to ensure security, peace and stability in the region.[114]

They formally agreed to deny access to third states who wished to use the region to launch military operations against any Caspian state, stating that "... they will not allow other countries to use their territories for acts of aggression or other military operations against any party."[115] The leaders of the Caspian Five have long made it clear that the presence of external forces in the Sea will not be tolerated, although the 2007 Summit declaration was the first time it was noted in a formal document. The declaration stated that only the littoral states were permitted to deploy ships and military forces in the sea, again seeking to limit the influence of external actors, particularly the United States and NATO. The declaration also provided for the development of nuclear energy for peaceful purposes and stated that the signatories bore "responsibility for damage inflicted on Caspian resources and to any Caspian state from the use of the Caspian Sea and development of its resources."[116] Despite being hailed by the Iranian president as a "turning point" in Caspian relations, there was no substantive change, and the 2007 declaration has proved to be little more than political rhetoric.

At the third Caspian summit held in Baku in 2010, a further 15-point declaration was signed, which included provision for multilateral cooperation on security issues, particularly environmental security, terrorism, organized crime, smuggling, trafficking, and illegal migration. One of the key points of the Agreement on Security Cooperation in the Caspian Sea was that the status of the Sea was to be determined only by the Caspian littoral countries, again highlighting the unwillingness of the Caspian Five to allow the involvement of any external actors. Russia and Iran are keen to ensure that they remain the dominant actors in the region and do not wish to see any third states, particularly the United States, establish any formal presence on the negotiating process over the Caspian's legal status. This reflects Russian (and Iranian) intolerance of any increased U.S./NATO presence in a region it considers to be its "sphere of privileged interest." Russia's response to suggestions that the United States may establish a presence at the Kazakh port of

Aqtau, as a means of getting its military equipment out of Afghanistan, highlighted its opposition to the presence of any external actors in the closed system of the Caspian Sea. An article in *Nezavisimaya Gazeta* argued that if Aqtau became a base for "the Pentagon and its allies," the "already fragile Caspian security architecture would effectively collapse."[117] In the article, Stanislav Pritchin from the Centre for the Study of Central Asia and the Caucasus warns that the presence of U.S. military personnel on the Caspian "will lead to an arms race in the region, particularly on the part of Russia and Iran."[118] Aleksandr Knyazev believes that both Russia and Iran have, until recently, "closed their eyes" to the U.S. presence in the region, particularly the American military support given to Azerbaijan and Kazakhstan in the development of their naval forces.[119]

As can be seen from the preceding paragraphs, there is very little security architecture in place in the Caspian region to actually "collapse." There is some, very minimal cooperation between the Caspian Five, particularly on environmental issues, but, on the whole, the Sea remains dominated by Russia and its sizeable military presence. The lukewarm response to the KASFOR initiative has not deterred Russia from seeking to boost military cooperation among the littoral states and, as discussed previously, there have been several joint and combined military exercises involving the Caspian states, but this cooperation is negligible. The CSTO held its first joint peacekeeping exercises in Kazakhstan in October 2012: *Nerush-imoye-bratstvo-2012* (Unbreakable brotherhood-2012) involved the establishment of a collective peacekeeping force in a Central Asian CSTO member-state experiencing "a crisis situation as a result of activities of international extremist and terrorist organizations, as well as disputes between ethnic groups."[120] This reflects concern across the region about possible instability emanating from Afghanistan in the wake of ISAF's withdrawal in 2014. Nevertheless, in spite of common concerns about instability from Afghanistan spilling over, unified action amongst the Caspian Five to mitigate any risk remains negligible, as the littoral states remain focused on national, rather than regional, solutions.

CONCLUSIONS AND RECOMMENDATIONS

Nearly 300 years old, the Caspian Flotilla has been undergoing an extensive upgrade, which has increased its capabilities significantly and signals Russian intent to remain the dominant power in the region: Moscow has firmly established its military dominance in the Caspian Sea, enhancing its maritime footprint and boosting its ability to shape the strategic environment. It is keen to secure its unstable "southern underbelly," and the Caspian Flotilla is intended to protect Russia's national interests and control a volatile region under threat from transnational security challenges, such as poaching, migration, a potential increase in drug trafficking as Afghanistan struggles to survive economically post-2014, and the movement of international extremist organizations. It is imperative to recognize Russia's sense of vulnerability on its southern periphery, which is the source of many security challenges, and also Russia's desire to remain the predominant power in the region, which has increased in significance since 1991 with the growing interest of external actors. Russia has strong historical, cultural, economic, and societal ties with the region and the "south" is one area where it remains the hegemon; no other state has yet established a presence to rival that of Russia.

The Caspian Sea has been vital for the security of Russia and its southern periphery since the 18th century. There are significant similarities between historical events and contemporary circumstances in the region, and the drivers of international interest in the Caspian Sea have changed little: the region's geostrategic significance, with Iran lying directly to the south, the vital importance of economic factors and maintaining access to natural resources, as well as lucrative trade routes, the competition for influence between different regional powers, and concern about the influence of external actors on the development of the region. Over the past few decades, the Caspian Sea has become pivotal for the United States (and the West), both in terms of its hydrocarbons, which provide an alternative source to Middle Eastern and Russian resources, and as an important transit route for the ISAF logistics operation. The decision to upgrade the Caspian Flotilla was made when Putin came to power at the beginning of 2000 and identified Russia's south, and the Caspian region, as an area of strategic interest.

The Russian narrative was (and remains) dominated by talk of "competition" and the need to be "competitive" with the West, which was perceived to be encroaching into an area that had previously been Moscow's exclusive zone of influence. The Caspian's natural resources, most notably its hydrocarbons, have led to the increased presence and influence of external actors, particularly from the United States and Europe, in a region that had been dominated by Russia for centuries. Oil and gas are the principal reasons for the interest of the West in the region, although the need to develop new transit routes in and out of Afghanistan has led to renewed interest in the region. Moscow has tolerated limited U.S. military support for Azerbaijan and Kazakhstan in terms of training and equipment support through the Caspian Guard initiative. However, the potential establishment of a transhipment base at Aqtau could exacerbate existing tensions in the region. Any such base developed on the Caspian Sea should be purely a civilian endeavor: the presence of U.S. military personnel and/or a U.S. military establishment in the region would be perceived as a provocative step by Moscow, which, as mentioned earlier, is determined to contain the influence of external actors. Russia is seeking to maintain the status quo in the Caspian Sea and ensure that its influence is not eroded by the appearance of actors from outside of the region, particularly by the U.S. and Western actors such as NATO. The United States should continue to develop its relations with states in the Caspian region, while acknowledging the significance of Russia's role in the region, as well as the sense of vulnerability it feels on its southern periphery.

The Caspian Sea is a unique area in several respects: its abundant natural resources, the lack of clear legal status, the growing presence and influence of external actors, and Russia's relations with its neighbors. Russia does not have complete sovereignty over the Caspian Sea: it shares responsibility for governing the area with four other states, three of which are former Soviet states, making it harder for Moscow to influence and shape the environment to its liking. The region is also where Russia faces significant challenges to its national interests from transnational threats, such as terrorism, insurgency, poaching, and smuggling. This is reflected in the upgrade of the Caspian Flotilla, which has acquired a number of new vessels designed to operate in shallow littoral waters, rather than blue-water operations, and conduct low-intensity maritime security operations such as the protection of Russian shipping and Russian offshore hydrocarbon production facilities, as well as monitoring the extraction of hydrocarbons and bio-resources in disputed areas of the Sea. The Flotilla's upgrade highlights the sense of vulnerability Russia feels in its south: stability and predictability are core concerns for Russia in the Caspian region and it is seeking to assert its control over the area to ensure these objectives. The new equipment being procured for the Flotilla is both defensive and offensive: the stealth capabilities would suggest an offensive posture, while the BAL coastal missile system is clearly defensive. The improvements to the Flotilla's capabilities are also indicative of how well Russia is reconfiguring its armed forces to tackle the security challenges of the 21st century.

For the three "new" states in the Caspian, particularly Azerbaijan and Kazakhstan, hydrocarbon reserves in the Sea are vital for their economic growth and future development (and ultimately long-term survival). All three have considerable hydrocarbon reserves and hope to become major players on the world energy market. Furthermore, their extensive hydrocarbon reserves have stimulated a lot of international interest and increased the presence of external actors in the Caspian region. However, even if they increase the production of hydrocarbons, they still face several enduring obstacles: the difficulty of transporting products from the remote, landlocked Caspian region to lucrative international markets and the unclarified legal status of the Sea. The lack of clarity about the Sea's legal status and the type of legal regime that should govern the maritime space represents the biggest impediment to stability in the region, creating uncertainty and political disagreement among states.

There is a need to encourage prompt resolution of the protracted dispute, although Iran is unlikely to agree to anything until it has fully explored its sector of the Sea, which may (or may not) contain significant quantities of oil and gas. As discussed earlier, the continuing lack of consensus between the Caspian Five about the Sea's legal status impacts upon maritime navigation, environmental protection, development of hydrocarbon potential, and the construction of new pipelines.

The Caspian littoral states have long recognized the need to develop infrastructure to transport their resources to international markets without relying on any one country, leading to investment in new pipelines such as the BTC, as well as the KCTS. But these projects have been fraught with geopolitical significance and have irritated Russia, who has been bypassed. This has eroded its influence over pipelines and export infrastructure in the Caspian Basin over the past decade, which has had both an economic and political impact: Moscow has lost out on revenue from transit tariffs, but has also seen its political dominance undermined. Nevertheless, the United States and its allies should continue to encourage the development of hydrocarbon transit infrastructure that circumvents Russian territory—Moscow already has far too much influence over oil and gas exports from the region, undermining the political and economic autonomy of states, particularly Kazakhstan and Azerbaijan. While these two states have so far managed to balance successfully their relations with Moscow and the West, their growing economic might will attract greater regional and international interest. They will need to upgrade their naval capabilities to be able to protect their economic interests and sea lines of communication in the Caspian and demonstrate intent. By contrast, Russia and Iran appear to be seeking to use their expanding naval capabilities to maintain the status quo in the Caspian Sea region, which is to their own advantage, and deter other littoral states from developing effective relationships with external actors. This desire to limit the influence and presence of external actors, especially the United States, and ensure their own dominance in the region undermines the sovereignty of the other littoral states and their ability to pursue an autonomous foreign policy. This desire also has significant implications for states outside the region, such as the United States, who wish to deepen their engagement with, and influence on, the Caspian states. Russian-Iranian relations in the Caspian Sea region will likely provide an indicator of the direction of broader relations between the two and should be monitored, since their burgeoning cooperation currently is being developed merely for mutual convenience, the establishment of a strategic partnership or alliance could be detrimental for U.S. influence in the future.

Despite bilateral cooperation, the Caspian Five have so far failed to establish any effective form of collective security system, and the region's security architecture is very weak. There have been some attempts to establish multilateral cooperation, but little has been achieved other than political declarations. The United States should encourage the development of some form of regional security system in the Caspian Sea area, to ensure that the littoral states take responsibility for regional security without the involvement of external actors. A collective security arrangement involving all five littoral states would also hinder any one regional state from becoming too dominant. The development of scientific, technical, and academic links with the region should be fostered, particularly in the areas of maritime environmental protection, the mitigation and management of oil spills and fisheries management.

The Caspian region is part of Russia's "southern underbelly," a term that underscores the sense of vulnerability it feels along its southern border—an area that is vital for Russian national security—both in terms of its natural resources and as a source of an array of security challenges. Moscow considers the broader Caspian region to be a sphere of its exclusive influence and has sought to counterbalance the growing involvement of other actors in the region, which has led to rising tension between Russia and its southern neighbors. While it is concerned about nontraditional security threats, Russia is also seeking to remain the predominant power in the Caspian Sea region. The upgrade of the Flotilla's capabilities is a visible signal of intent that Russia is unwilling to cede any further influence and intends to remain the predominant power in the Caspian Sea region.

BIBLIOGRAPHY

Akiner, Shirin (ed.), *The Caspian: Politics, Energy and Security,* Abingdon, UK: RoutledgeCurzon, 2004.

ANS TV, Baku, 1600GMT, August 8, 2003, BBC Monitoring Select Middle East, August 15, 2003, p. 3.

Azernews, "Work on Caspian Sea draft convention progressing," November 25, 2013, available from *www.azernews.az/azerbaijan/61886.html.*

Barabanov, Mikhail, A New Fleet for Russia — An Independent Vision," *The Journal of Slavic Military Studies*, Vol. 24, No. 1, 2011, pp. 81-87.

Binnie, Jeremy, "All at sea: Iran threatens military moves into the Caspian," *Jane's Intelligence Review*, September 24, 2012.

Bisenbaev, Asyilbek, *Nye vmeste: Rossiya i stranyi Tsentralnoi Azii (Not together: Russia and the Central Asian states),* Moscow, Russia: Piter, 2011.

BP Statistical Review of World Energy, June 2013, available from *www.bp.com.*

Brilev, Sergei, "Sergei Shoigu: nasha armiya dolzhna ponyat," na chto sposobna," ("Sergei Shoigu: Our Army Needs to Understand What Is Possible"), *Vesti,* November 9, 2013 available from *www.vesti.ru/doc.html?id=1152052.*

The Constitution of the Republic of Azerbaijan, adopted November 12, 1995, by popular referendum, available from *en.president. az/azerbaijan/constitution/.*

"Caspian Guard," available from *www.globalsecurity.org/military/ops/caspian-guard.htm.*

Dunai, Peter, "Russia delays bulk of new armament spend until 2016, *Jane's Defence Weekly,* October 8, 2012.

Emirov, RM, *Prioritetyi natsional"noi bezopastnosti Rossiiskoi Federatsii na Severnom Kavkaze* (*The Russian Federation's National Security Priorities in the North Caucasus*), Moscow, Russia: Logos, 2011.

EU Energy Security and Solidarity Action Plan: Second Strategic Energy Review, European Commission, Directorate-General for Energy and Transport, Brussels, 2008, available from *ec.europa.eu/ energy/strategies/2008/2008_11_ser2_en.htm*.

Fish, Tim, "Russian navy to axe half its ships by 2016," *Jane's Navy International*, March 6, 2009.

The Foreign Policy Concept of the Russian Federation, Approved by Dmitry Medvedev, President of the Russian Federation on July 12, 2008, available from *www.mid.ru/ns-osndoc.nsf/1e5f0de2 8fe77fdcc32575d900298676/869c9d2b87ad8014c32575d9002b1c38? OpenDocument*.

The Foreign Policy Concept of the Russian Federation, Approved by Vladimir Putin, President of the Russian Federation on February 12, 2013, available from *www.mid.ru/bdomp/ns-osndoc.nsf/1e5f 0de28fe77fdcc32575d900298676/869c9d2b87ad8014c32575d9002b1c3 8!OpenDocument*.

Gordeyev, Mariya, "China buys in giant Kazakh oilfield for $5 billion," September 7, 2013.

Gyürösi, Miroslav, "Kazakhstan studies Exocet as coastal defence weapon," *Jane's Missiles & Rockets*, September 3, 2012.

Hafizoglu, Rufiz, "Azerbaijani Energy Ministry announces transit volumes of Kazakh oil for 2014," *Trend news agency*, December 2, 2013, available from *en.trend.az/capital/energy/ 2217306.html*.

Harmer, Christopher, "Iranian Naval and Maritime Strategy," *Middle East Security Report 12*, Washington, DC: Institute for the Study of War, June 2013.

Interfax-AVN military news agency, Moscow, 0701GMT, September 25, 2012, BBC Monitoring.

Interfax-AVN military news agency, Moscow, 1339GMT, September 17, 2012, BBC Monitoring.

Interfax-AVN military news agency, Moscow, 1026GMT, October 3, 2012, BBC Monitoring.

Interfax-AVN military news agency, Moscow, 1305GMT, November 6, 2012, BBC Monitoring.

Ivlent'eva, T, "V gosudarstvennoy morskoy inspektsii. Brakon"yry ozloblyayutsya i vooruzhayutsya" ("State Maritime Inspectorate: Poachers Resentful and Arming Themselves"), *Kaspiets*, April 11, 2002, BBC Monitoring.

Ivanov, Andrei and Shulman, Aleksandr, "Will Hamas come to the Caucasus?" *Svpressa.ru*, November 19, 2012, available from *www.svpressa.ru/war21/article/60975/*.

Izvestiya, March 31, 2008, online version available from *www. izvestiya.ru*.

Jacobs, Keith, "Russian Navy Quo Vadis?" *Naval Forces*, Vol. 3, 2009, pp. 56-63.

Jane's Foreign Report (online version), "Striking energy gold in the Caspian," December 15, 2008.

Jane's Islamic Affairs Analyst, "Looking to 2020: Azerbaijan's military aspirations," April 23, 2008.

Janusz, Barbara, *The Caspian Sea Legal Status and Regime Problems*, Briefing Paper, REP BP 05/02, London, UK: The Royal Institute of International Affairs, August 2005.

Kapitanets, IM, *Voina na more: aktual'nyie problemyi razvitiya voenno-morskoi nauki (War at Sea: Pressing Problems with the Development of Maritime Theory)* Moscow, Russia: VAGRIUS, 2001.

Karami, Jahangir, "The Collective Security System in the Caspian Sea. Opportunities, restrictions and future perspective," *Caspian Factor,* Institute for Caspian Cooperation, May 30, 2013.

Karimi, Nasser, "Jamaran-2, Iran Destroyer, Launched In the Caspian Sea," *Huffington Post*, March 17, 2013, available from *www.huffingtonpost.com/2013/03/17/jamaran-2-destroyer-iran-caspian-sea_n_2895553.html*.

Kaspiyets, Astrakhan,September 28, 2012, BBC Monitoring.

Keneş, Bülent, "We must stop seeing Azerbaijan purely as a source of oil and natural gas," *Today's Zaman*, October 4, 2012, available from *www.todayszaman.com/columnist/bulent-kenes-294 312-we-must-stop-seeing-azerbaijan-purely-as-a-source-of-oil-and-natural-gas.html*.

Khramchikhin, Aleksandr, "'Tsentr'priblizilsya k okrainam" ("'Centre' Closer to Regions"), *Nezavisimoye Voyennoye Obozreniye*, 7.10.11, available from *nvo.ng.ru/maneuvers/2011-10-07/1_center.html*.

Konyrova, Kulpash, "Kazakhstan Caspian Transport System Project Postponed," June 27, 2010, *New Europe Online*, available from *www.neurope.eu/article/kazakhstan-caspian-transport-system-project-postponed*.

Kucera, Joshua, "Kazakhstan unveils "first" home-grown patrol ship," *Jane's Navy International*, April 20, 2012.

Kucera, Josh, "Turkmenistan: Ashgabat Quietly Builds Up Caspian Military Might," *Eurasianet.org*, July 5, 2012, available from *www.eurasianet.org/node/65633*.

Kuzin, VP and Nikolskii, VI, *Voenno-morskoi flot SSSR 1945-1991 (The Soviet Navy 1945-1991)*, St Petersburg, Russia: Istoricheskoye Morskoye Obshchestvo, 1996.

Laruelle, Marlene and Peyrouse, Sebastien, "The Militarisation of the Caspian Sea: 'Great Games' and 'Small Games' over the Caspian Fleets," *China and Eurasia Forum Quarterly*, Vol. 7, No. 2, 2009, pp. 17-35.

Main, Dr. Steven J., *The Bear, the Peacock, the Eagle, the Sturgeon and the Black, Black Oil: Contemporary Regional Power Politics in the Caspian Sea*, Caucasus Series 05/67, Shrivenham, UK: Conflict Studies Research Centre, December 2005.

Makovskiy, AA and Radchenko, BM, *Kaspiyskaya krasnoznamennaya (The Red Banner in the Caspian)*, Moscow, Russia: Voenizdat, 1982.

Malashenko, Aleksei, *Tsentralnaya Asiya: na shto rasschityivaet Rossiya? (Central Asia and Russia's Expectations)*, Moscow, Russia: Tsentr Carnegie, 2012.

Malyisheva, Dina, "Vyivod voisk mezhdunarodnoi koalitsii iz Afghanistana i Tsentralnaya Aziya" ("The Withdrawal of International Coalition Troops from Afghanistan and Central Asia"), *Otsenki i idei*, Vol. 1, No. 2, Moscow, Russia: Institute Vostokovedeniya RAN, August 2012.

Maruev, A. Iu and Karpenko, A. O., "Voenno-politicheskie aspekty formirovaniia interesov Rossii na yuzhnom geopoliticheskom vektore" ("Military-Political Aspects of the Formation of Russia's Interests in the Southern Geopolitical Vector"), *Voennaya Mysl,*" No. 11, November 2009, pp. 9-16.

Mazumdar, Mrityunjoy, "Turkmenistan acquires Its first surface combatants," *Jane's Navy International*, September 30, 2011.

McDermott, Roger, "Kazakhstan-Russia: enduring Eurasian defence partners," *Danish Institute for International Studies Report*, Copenhagen, Denmark: Institute for International Studies, 2012, p. 15.

Mehr News Agency, Tehran, 0510GMT, March 13, 2010, BBC Monitoring.

The Military Doctrine of the Republic of Kazakhstan, Presidential Decree, No. 161, October 11, 2001.

The Military Doctrine of the Russian Federation, approved by decree of the President of the Russian Federation on February 5, 2010, available from *www.scrf.gov.ru/documents/33.html.*

Ministerstvo oboronyi Rossiiskoi Federatsii (The Ministry of Defense of the Russian Federation), "Na Kaspiiskoi flotillii formiruyot ekipazhi dlya noveishikh malyikh raketnyikh korablei" ("Crews Assembled for Caspian Flotilla's New Small Rocket Ships"), November 1, 2012, available from *function.mil.ru/ news_page/country/more.htm?id=11438895@egNews.*

Ministerstvo oboronyi Rossiiskoi Federatsii, "Kaspiiskaya flotiliya: istoriya" ("The Caspian Flotilla: A History"), available from *structure.mil.ru/structure/forces/type/navy/kasp/history.htm.*

Ministerstvo oboronyi Rossiiskoi Federatsii, "Moryaki Kaspiiskoi flotilii ostaivayut noviy mnogotselevoi korabl" ("Caspian Flotilla Sailors Acquaint Themselves with New Multirole Ships"), August 2, 2013, available from *function.mil.ru/news_page/country/ more.htm?id=11810634@egNews.*

Ministerstvo oboronyi Rossiiskoi Federatsii, "Korabli Kaspiiskoi flotilii v khode ucheniya proveli vstrechnyi morskoi boi" ("Caspian Flotilla Ships Conduct Sea Battle during Exercises"), August 16, 2013, available from *function.mil.ru/news_page/country/ more.htm?id=11820011@egNews.*

Morskaya doktrina Rossiiskoi Federatsii na period do 2020 goda (*Maritime Doctrine of the Russian Federation for the Period until 2020*), approved by Vladimir Putin, President of the Russian Federation on July 27, 2001, available from *www.scrf.gov.ru/documents/34.html.*

"Russia may resume sturgeon fishing," *The Moscow Times,* July 6, 2012, available from *www.themoscowtimes.com/special/ environment/eng/russia-may-resume-sturgeon-fishing.html.*

Mukhtarov, D., "Kazakh and Russian border guards join in fight against Caspian Sea poachers," October 11, 2013, *Trend News Agency,* available from *en.trend.az/regions/casia/kazakhstan/ 2200390.html.*

Murphy, Daniel T, "Russia's world turned upside down," *US Naval Institute Proceedings,* May 2012, Vol. 138, Issue 5, pp. 54-59.

National Security Strategy of the Russian Federation, approved by decree of the President of the Russian Federation, May 12, 2009, available from *www.scrf.gov.ru/documents/1/99.html.*

Nekhai, Oleg, "Caspian Sea stocks to be restored," *Voice of Russia* Radio, May 3, 2013, available from *voiceofrussia.com/2013_05_03/Caspian-Sea-sturgeon-stocks-to-be-restored/.*

Nezavisimaya Gazeta, August 16, 1997.

Nezavisimaya Gazeta, November 22, 2011, available from *www.ng.ru/economics/2011-11-22/1_kaspiy.html.*

Oldberg, Ingmar, *The Russian Navy facing the 21st century: proceedings of a conference in Stockholm,* December 2, 1996, Stockholm, Sweden: Swedish Defense Research Establishment, Defense Research Establishment, 1997.

Orujova, Nigar, "First sturgeon farm to open in Azerbaijan," *Azernews,* November 7, 2013, available from *www.azernews.az/azerbaijan/61392.html.*

Orujova, Nigar, "Azerbaijan to build warships in 2014," *Azernews,* November 12, 2013, available from *www.azernews.az/azerbaijan/61533.html.*

Panfilova, Viktoriya, "Na Kaspii sozdayetsya voenno-morskaya baza SShA" ("USA to Establish Naval Base on Caspian"), April 29, 2013, available from *www.ng.ru/cis/2013-04-29/6_kaspiy.html.*

Pannier, Bruce, "Caspian dispute casts shadow over Nabucco," *Asia Times Online,* July 30, 2009, available from *www.atimes.com/atimes/Central_Asia/KG30Ag01.html.*

Patsuria, Nino, "Kazakh oil secures BTC volumes," *Georgia News,* November 7, 2013.

Pivovar, EI, *Rossiisko-azerbaidzhanskie otnosheniya: konets XX-nachalo XXI veka* (*Russian-Azerbaijani Relations from the End of the 20th to the Beginning of the 21st Centuries*), Moscow, Russia: Kremlin Multimedia, 2012.

Press TV, "Iran launches indigenous Jamaran 2 destroyer in Caspian Sea," March 17, 2013, available from *www.presstv.com/detail/2013/03/17/294010/iran-launches-jamaran-2-destroyer/*.

Press TV, "Iranian naval group docked in Astrakhan carries message of peace, envoy says," June 28, 2013, available from *www.presstv.com/detail/2013/06/28/311292/iran-naval-group-carries-message-of-peace/*.

Putin, Vladimir, Speech by the President of the Russian Federation, "Komandno-shtabnyie ucheniye 'Kavkaz-2012'" ("Command Post Exercise 'Kavkaz-2012'"), 17.9.11, available from *kremlin.ru/transcripts/16492*.

Putin, Vladimir, "Presidential Address to the Federal Assembly," December 12, 2013, available from *eng.kremlin.ru/news/6402*.

Radio Free Europe Radio Liberty, "Turkmenistan Plans Caspian Naval Base," August 31, 2009, available from *www.rferl.org/content/Turkmenistan_Plans_Caspian_Naval_Base/1811441.html*.

Radio Free Europe Radio Liberty, "Kazakh Border Guards Kill Suspected Russian Poacher," November 26, 2013, available from 2013.

Reuters news agency, "Kazakh head reshuffles oil officials after Kashagan delays," July 3, 2013.

RIA Novosti, "Caspian states adopt declaration on repelling aggressors," October 16, 2007, available from *en.rian.ru/world/20071016/84185487.html*.

RIA Novosti, "Putin kicks off oil project on Caspian Sea" April 28, 2010.

RIA Novosti, "New Russian Missile Boat Starts Caspian Trials," August 6, 2013, available from *rusnavy.com/news/newsofday/index.php?ELEMENT_ID=17033*.

Rossiskaya Gazeta, Moscow, Russia, 0850GMT, August 30, 2012, BBC Monitoring.

Rusnavy.com, "New Super-Frigate to Protect Caspian Sea," June 8, 2012, available from *rusnavy.com/news/navy/index.php?ELEMENT_ID=15315.*

Russia Today, "Iran claims $50bln oil field found in Caspian Sea," July 16, 2012, available from *rt.com/business/iran-claims-vast-oil-field-found-in-caspian-sea-302/.*

Sadykov, Murat, "Russia Concerned About Caspian Ecosystem, When Expedient," *Eurasianet.org,* November 26, 2013, available from *www.eurasianet.org/node/67800.*

Saivetz, Carol R., "Putin's Caspian Policy," Policy Brief, Caspian Studies Program, October 2000, Cambridge, MA: John F. Kennedy School of Government, Belfer Center for Science and International Affairs, available from *belfercenter.hks.harvard.edu/publication/3101/putins_caspian_policy.html.*

Shakleina, T. A., *Rossiya i SShA v mirovoi politike (Russia and the USA in Global Politics),* Moscow, Russia: Aspekt Press, 2012.

Tehran Times, "Iran's oil deposits in Caspian Sea worth over $50bn," July 9, 2012, available from *tehrantimes.com/economy-and-business/99479-irans-oil-deposits-in-caspian-sea-worth-over-50b.*

Tringham, Kate, "Almaz launches third Buyan-class gunboat," *Jane's Navy International,* May 2, 2012.

"Turkmenistan: Naval Forces," available from *www.globalsecurity.org/military/world/centralasia/turkmen-navy.htm.*

Today.az, "EU satisfied with auspicious conditions for Trans-Caspian Gas Pipeline conclusion," November 20, 2013, available from *www.today.az/news/business/128353.html.*

Uc Noqta, Baku, June 19, 2003, Select Central Asian and Transcaucasus, BBC Monitoring, June 19, 2003, p. 21.

U.S. Department of State, Office of the Coordinator for Counterterrorism, "Chapter 2. Country Reports: Europe and Eurasia Overview," *Country Reports on Terrorism 2011*, Washington, DC: U.S. Department of State, July 31, 2012, available from *www.state.gov/j/ct/rls/crt/2011/195543.htm*.

U.S. Energy Information Administration, "Kazakhstan Country Analysis Brief," Washington, DC: U.S. Energy Information Administration, available from *www.eia.gov/countries/cab.cfm?fips=KZ*.

U.S. Energy Information Administration, "Turkmenistan Country Analysis Brief," Washington, DC: U.S. Energy Information Administration, available from *www.eia.gov/countries/cab.cfm?fips=TX*.

Ustinov, Evgenii, "Bioterrorizm: mesto deystviy – Kaspiy" ("Bioterrorism in Action in the Caspian), *Krasnaya Zvezda*, June 25, 2004.

Voyennyy Vestnik Yuga Rossii (*Military Bulletin of Southern Russia*), Rostov-na-Donu, September 29, 2012, BBC Monitoring.

Zhil'tsov, SS, Zoni, IS, and Ushkov, AM, *Geopolitika kaspiiskogo regiona* (*The Geopolitics of the Caspian Region*), Moscow, Russia: mezhdunarodnayie otnosheniya, 2003.

Zvezda TV, Moscow, 1800GMT, October 24, 2012, BBC Monitoring.

INTERVIEWS

Interviews and informal conversations were conducted with representatives of the following institutions in Moscow, Russia, and Astana and Almaty (Kazakhstan).

Russia.

The Centre for Regional Problems, USA and Canada Institute (ISKRAN), Moscow.
The Carnegie Centre, Moscow.
The Department of Central Asia and Kazakhstan, CIS Institute, Moscow.

Kazakhstan.

The Ministry of Defense Astana.
The Centre for Military and Strategic Research, Astana.
The Kazakhstan Institute for Strategic Studies, Almaty.

ENDNOTES

1. Ministerstvo oboronyi Rossiiskoi Federatsii, "Kaspiiskaya flotiliya: istoriya'," ("The Caspian Flotilla: A History"), November 1, 2012, available from *structure.mil.ru/structure/forces/type/navy/kasp/history.htm*.

2. See A. Iu Maruev and A. O. Karpenko, "Voenno-politicheskie aspekty formirovaniia interesov Rossii na yuzhnom geopoliticheskom vektore" ("Military-Political Aspects of the Formation of Russia's Interests in the Southern Geopolitical Vector"), *Voennaya Mysl'*, No. 11, November 2009, p. 9.

3. S. S. Zhil'tsov, I. S. Zoni, and A. M. Ushkov, *Geopolitika kaspiiskogo regiona* (*The Geopolitics of the Caspian Region*), Moscow, Russia: mezhdunarodnayie otnosheniya, 2003, p. 110.

4. Russian successes, such as the subsea Blue Stream gas pipeline, are considered to be the result of the "failure of American pipeline strategy in the Caucasus and Central Asia as a whole," *Ibid.*, p. 131.

5. See *www.portaktau.kz/eng/AktauPort/today/*.

6. Viktoriya Panfilova, "Na Kaspii sozdayetsya voenno-morskaya baza SShA" ("USA to Establish Naval Base on Caspian"), April 29, 2013, available from *www.ng.ru/cis/2013-04-29/6_kaspiy.html*.

7. A. A. Makovskiy and B. M. Radchenko, *Kaspiyskaya krasno-znamennaya* (*The Red Banner in the Caspian*), Moscow, Russia: Voenizdat, 1982, p. 3.

8. *Ibid.*

9. *Ibid.*, pp. 5-6.

10. The Ottoman Empire dominated the western side of the contemporary South Caucasus from the 16th century until the early-20th century; until the beginning of the 19th century, many areas of the Caucasus were part of the Persian Empire.

11. *Morskaya doktrina Rossiiskoi Federatsii na period do 2020 goda (Maritime Doctrine of the Russian Federation for the Period until 2020)* approved by Vladimir Putin, President of the Russian Federation, on July 27, 2001, p. 7, available from *www.scrf.gov.ru/documents/ 34.html*.

12. *Ibid.*, pp. 9-10.

13. Figures taken from *BP Statistical Review of World Energy,* June 2013, available from *www.bp.com*. Reserves-to-production (R/P) ratio – "if the reserves remaining at the end of any year are divided by the production in that year, the result is the length of time that those remaining reserves would last if production were to continue at that rate," *BP Statistical Review of World Energy*, p. 6.

14. For further details, see "Kazakhstan Country Analysis Brief," Washington, DC: U.S. Energy Information Administration, available from *www.eia.gov/countries/cab.cfm?fips=KZ*.

15. See *www.tengizchevroil.com/*.

16. See *www.kpo.kz/kpobv-home.html?&L=0*.

17. "Kazakh head reshuffles oil officials after Kashagan delays," *Reuters* news agency, July 3, 2013, available from *www. reuters.com/article/2013/07/03/oil-kazakhstan-minister-idUSL5N- 0F90RC20130703*.

18. "Mariya Gordeyev, "China buys in giant Kazakh oilfield for $5 billion," September 7, 2013, available from *www.reuters.com/ article/2013/09/07/us-oil-kashagan-china-idUSBRE98606620130907*.

19. *Ibid.* According to Kazakh president Nursultan Nazarbayev, a total of 22 agreements worth U.S.$30 billion were

signed during Xi's visit, including one to build an oil refinery in Kazakhstan.

20. For further details, see BP Caspian, available from *www. bp.com/en_az/caspian.html*.

21. *Ibid.*

22. For further details see BP Caspian, available from *www. bp.com/sectiongenericarticle.do?categoryId=9048303&content Id=7015092*.

23. The audit, conducted by a UK consultancy firm Gaffney, Cline & Associates, put the best-case volume of gas at South Yolo-tan-Osman at six trillion cubic meters (Tcm), but said there could be as much as 14 Tcm. "Striking energy gold in the Caspian," *Jane's Foreign Report* (online version), December 15, 2008.

24. For further details, see "Turkmenistan Country Analysis Brief," Washington, DC: U.S. Energy Information Administration, available from *www.eia.gov/countries/cab.cfm?fips=TX*.

25. See *RIA Novosti*, "Putin kicks off oil project on Caspian Sea," April 28, 2010, available from *en.rian.ru/russia/ 20100428/158790351.html*.

26. "Iran's oil deposits in Caspian Sea worth over $50bn," *Tehran Times*, July 9, 2012, available from *tehrantimes.com/economy-and-business/99479-irans-oil-deposits-in-caspian-sea-worth-over-50b*.

27. "Iran claims $50bln oil field found in Caspian Sea," *Russia Today*, July 16, 2012, available from *rt.com/business/iran-claims-vast-oil-field-found-in-caspian-sea-302/*.

28. Quoted in *Nezavisimaya Gazeta*, August 16, 1997.

29. The first cargo of oil transported through the pipeline was exported from Ceyhan in June 2006.

30. Turkmenistan has exported some crude through the BTC. According to a report published in December 2013, to date, about 8.6 million tons of Turkmen oil has been transported through

the pipeline. Rufiz Hafizoglu, "Azerbaijani Energy Ministry announces transit volumes of Kazakh oil for 2014," *Trend News Agency*, December 2, 2013, available from *en.trend.az/capital/energy/2217306.html*.

31. Nino Patsuria, "Kazakh oil secures BTC volumes," *Georgia News*, November 7, 2013, available from *www.georgianews.ge/business/25236-kazakh-oil-secures-btc-volumes.html*.

32. See *www.kmg.kz*.

33. Kulpash Konyrova, "Kazakhstan Caspian Transport System Project Postponed," June 27, 2010, *New Europe Online*, available from *www.neurope.eu/article/kazakhstan-caspian-transport-system-project-postponed*.

34. Rufiz Hafizoglu, "Azerbaijani Energy Ministry announces transit volumes of Kazakh oil for 2014," *Trend news agency*, December 2, 2013, available from *en.trend.az/capital/energy/2217306.html*.

35. Zhil'tsov *et al.*, p. 110.

36. *Ibid.*, p. 131.

37. *Izvestiya*, 31.3.08, online version available from *www.izvestiya.ru*. International oil prices jumped over U.S.$1.70 per barrel because of fears of supply disruption due to the military conflict in South Ossetia. Brent crude was trading at U.S.$115.10 in London on August 11, 2008, up from U.S.$113.33 on August 8, while Nymex crude rose U.S.$1.16 to U.S.$116.36.

38. *EU Energy Security and Solidarity Action Plan: Second Strategic Energy Review*, European Commission, Brussels, Belgium: Directorate-General for Energy and Transport, 2008, available from *ec.europa.eu/energy/strategies/2008/2008_11_ser2_en.htm*.

39. "EU satisfied with auspicious conditions for Trans-Caspian Gas Pipeline conclusion," November 20, 2013, *Today.az*, available from *www.today.az/news/business/128353.html*.

40. *Murat Sadykov,* "Russia Concerned About Caspian Ecosystem, When Expedient," *Eurasianet.org,* November 26, 2013, available from *www.eurasianet.org/node/67800.*

41. Quoted in *Nezavisimaya Gazeta,* November 22, 2011, available from *www.ng.ru/economics/2011-11-22/1_kaspiy.html.*

42. Evgenii Ustinov, "Bioterrorizm: mesto deystviya – Kaspiy," *Krasnaya Zvezda* ("Bioterrorism in Action in the Caspian"), June 25, 2004, available from *old.redstar.ru/2004/06/25_06/3_02.html.*

43. Including the huso and starred sturgeon. See Oleg Nekhai, "Caspian Sea stocks to be restored," *Voice of Russia* Radio, May 3, 2013, available from *voiceofrussia.com/2013_05_03/Caspian-Sea-sturgeon-stocks-to-be-restored/;* and Nigar Orujova, "First sturgeon farm to open in Azerbaijan," *Azernews,* November 7, 2013, available from *www.azernews.az/azerbaijan/61392.html.*

44. *Ibid.*

45. "Russia may resume sturgeon fishing," July 6, 2012, *The Moscow Times,* available from *www.themoscowtimes.com/special/environment/eng/russia-may-resume-sturgeon-fishing.html.*

46. D. Mukhtarov, "Kazakh and Russian border guards join in fight against Caspian Sea poachers," October 11, 2013, *Trend News Agency,* available from *en.trend.az/regions/casia/kazakhstan/2200390.html.*

47. "Kazakh Border Guards Kill Suspected Russian Poacher," *Radio Free Europe Radio Liberty,* November 26, 2013, available from *www.rferl.org/content/kazakhstan-poaching-russia/25180778.html.*

48. T. Ivlent'eva, "V gosudarstvennoy morskoy inspektsii. Brakon'yry ozloblyayutsya i vooruzhayutsya" ("State Maritime Inspectorate: Poachers Resentful and Arming Themselves"), *Kaspiets,* April 11, 2002; "Putin sets out vision for development of Caspian oil fields," BBC Monitoring, April 25, 2002 quoted in Dr. Steven J. Main, *The Bear, the Peacock, the Eagle, the Sturgeon and the Black, Black Oil: Contemporary Regional Power Politics in the Caspian Sea,* Caucasus Series 05/67, Shrivenham, UK: Conflict Studies Research Centre, December 2005.

49. Quoted in EI Pivovar, *Rossiisko-azerbaidzhanskie otnosheni-ya: konets XX-nachalo XXI veka (Russian-Azerbaijani Relations from the End of the 20th to the Beginning of the 21st Centuries)*, Moscow, Russia: Kremlin Multimedia, 2012, p. 131.

50. Bruce Pannier, "Caspian dispute casts shadow over Na-bucco," *Asia Times Online*, July 30, 2009, available from *www.atimes.com/atimes/Central_Asia/KG30Ag01.html*.

51.*The Constitution of the Republic of Azerbaijan*, adopted November 12, 1995, by popular referendum, Article 11, para. 2, available from *en.president.az/azerbaijan/constitution/*.

52. Maruev and Karpenko, p. 9.

53. *Russia's National Security Strategy to 2020*, paras. 11 and 12, 2009.

54. *Ibid.*, para. 42.

55. Sergei Brilev, "Sergei Shoigu: nasha armiya dolzhna po-nyat," na chto sposobna," ("Sergei Shoigu: Our Army Needs to Understand What Is Possible"), *Vesti*, November 9, 2013, available from *www.vesti.ru/doc.html?id=1152052*.

56. Andrei Ivanov and Aleksandr Shulman, "Khamas pridyot na Kavkaz?" ("Hamas in the Caucasus?"), *Svpressa.ru*, November 19, 2012, available from *www.svpressa.ru/war21/article/60975/*.

57. Quoted in Saivetz, "Putin's Caspian Policy."

58. Maruev and Karpenko, p. 9.

59. Kaspiiskaya flotiliya: istoriya.

60. Mevluk Katik, "Militarisation of the Caspian Sea," Shirin Akiner, ed., *The Caspian: Politics, Energy and Security*, Abingdon, UK: RoutledgeCurzon, 2004, p. 300.

61. Tim Fish, "Russian navy to axe half its ships by 2016," *Jane's Navy International*, June 3, 2009.

62. Figures quoted in Daniel T. Murphy, "Russia's World Turned Upside Down," *U.S. Naval Institute Proceedings,* May 2012, Vol. 138, Issue 5, pp. 54-59. This is a significant amount, relying on continuing high oil and gas prices.

63. Peter Dunai, "Russia delays bulk of new armament spend until 2016," *Jane's Defence Weekly,* October 8, 2012.

64. "New Super-Frigate to Protect Caspian Sea," June 8, 2012, available from *rusnavy.com/news/navy/index.php?ELEMENT_ID= 15315.*

65. Report on *Zvezda TV,* controlled by the Russian Ministry of Defense, BBC Monitoring, Zvezda TV, Moscow, 1800GMT, October 24, 2012.

66. Kate Tringham, "Almaz launches third Buyan-class gunboat," *Jane's Navy International,* May 2, 2012.

67. BBC Monitoring, *Rossiskaya Gazeta* website, Moscow, 0850GMT, October 30, 2012.

68. Ministerstvo oboronyi Rossiiskoi Federatsii, "Na Kaspiiskoi flotillii formiruyot ekipazhi dlya noveishikh malyikh raketnyikh korablei" ('Crews Assembled for Caspian Flotilla's New Small Rocket Ships"), November 1, 2012, available from *function. mil.ru/news_page/country/more.htm?id=11438895@egNews.*

69. Ministerstvo oboronyi Rossiiskoi Federatsii, "Moryaki Kaspiiskoi flotilii ostaivayut noviy mnogotselevoi korabl" ("Caspian Flotilla Sailors Acquaint Themselves with New Multirole Ships"), August 2, 2013, pp. 13-34, available from *function.mil.ru/ news_page/country/more.htm?id=11438895@egNews.*

70. BBC Monitoring, *Interfax-AVN* military news agency, Moscow, 1305GMT, November 6, 2012.

71. BBC Monitoring, *Voyennyy Vestnik Yuga Rossii* (*Military Bulletin of Southern Russia*), Rostov-na-Donu, September 29, 2012.

72. "New Russian Missile Boat Starts Caspian Trials," *RIA Novosti,* August 6, 2013, available from *rusnavy.com/news/newsofday/ index.php?ELEMENT_ID=17033.*

73. BBC Monitoring, *Kaspiyets*, Astrakhan, September 28, 2012.

74. BBC Monitoring, *Interfax-AVN* military news agency, Moscow, 0701GMT, September 25, 2012.

75. BBC Monitoring, *Interfax-AVN* military news agency, Moscow, 1339GMT, September 17, 2012.

76. Speech by the President of the Russian Federation Vladimir Putin, "Komandno-shtabnyie ucheniye 'Kavkaz-2012'" ("Command Post Exercise 'Kavkaz-2012'"), September 17, 2011, available from *kremlin.ru/transcripts/16492*.

77. Russian Ministry of Defence website, "Korabli Kaspiiskoi flotilii v khode ucheniya proveli vstrechnyi morskoi boi" ("Caspian Flotilla Ships Conduct Sea Battle during Exercises"), August 16, 2013, (12:02), available from *function.mil.ru/news_page/country/more.htm?id=11820011@egNews*.

78. Mikhail Barabanov, "A New Fleet for Russia-An Independent Vision," *The Journal of Slavic Military Studies*, Vol. 24, No. 1, 2011, p. 84.

79. Aleksandr Khramchikhin, "'Tsentr' priblizilsya k okrainam" ("'Centre' Closer to Regions"), *Nezavisimoye Voyennoye Obozreniye*, July 10, 2011.

80. *Ibid.*

81. *Military Doctrine of the Republic of Kazakhstan*, President Decree, No. 161, October 11, 2001, available from *www.mod.gov.kz/mod-en/index.php/2009-06-26-02-25-27*.

82. Quoted in Roger McDermott, "Kazakhstan-Russia: enduring Eurasian defence partners," *Danish Institute for International Studies Report*, 15, Copenhagen, Denmark: Danish Institute for International Studies, 2012, p. 24.

83. Joshua Kucera, "Kazakhstan unveils 'first' home-grown patrol ship," *Jane's Navy International*, April 20, 2012.

84. *Ibid.*

85. Miroslav Gyürösi, "Kazakhstan studies Exocet as coastal defence weapon," *Jane's Missiles & Rockets*, September 3, 2012.

86. Nigar Orujova, "Azerbaijan to build warships in 2014," *Azernews*, November 12, 2013, available from *www.azernews.az/ azerbaijan/61533.html*.

87. For further details, see "Caspian Guard," available from *www.globalsecurity.org/military/ops/caspian-guard.htm*.

88. The 2003 Goplat exercises involved 18 U.S. servicemen and 45 Azeris, together with two Mi-8 helicopters and two coast-guard boats, seeking to protect oil and gas platforms. See BBC Monitoring Select Central Asia and Transcaucasus, June 19, 2003, p. 21; *Uc Noqta*, Baku, June 19, 2003, p. 3.

89. Spokesman Ezzatollah Jalali said the involvement of other countries posed a threat not only to Iran, but to the region as a whole. Azerbaijan responded by stating that the exercises were not directed against any country and that, as an independent sovereign country, it had the right to pursue its own policy. BBC Monitoring Select Middle East, August 15, 2003, p. 3; *ANS TV*, Baku, 1600GMT, August 14, 2003.

90. Jeremy Binnie, "All at sea: Iran threatens military moves into the Caspian," *Jane's Intelligence Review*, September 24, 2012.

91. Office of the Coordinator for Counterterrorism, "Chapter 2. Country Reports: Europe and Eurasia Overview," Washington, DC: Country Reports on Terrorism 2011, U.S. Department of State, July 31, 2012, available from *www.state.gov/j/ct/rls/crt/2011/ 195543.htm*.

92. "Looking to 2020: Azerbaijan's military aspirations," *Jane's Islamic Affairs Analyst*, April 23, 2008.

93. Bülent Keneş, "We must stop seeing Azerbaijan purely as a source of oil and natural gas," October 4, 2012.

94. "Turkmenistan: Naval Forces," available from *www.globalsecurity.org/military/world/centralasia/turkmen-navy.htm.*

95. Josh Kucera, "Turkmenistan: Ashgabat Quietly Builds Up Caspian Military Might," *Eurasianet.org*, July 5, 2012, available from *www.eurasianet.org/node/65633.*

96. Mrityunjoy Mazumdar, "Turkmenistan acquires its first surface combatants," *Jane's Navy International*, September 30, 2011.

97. "Turkmenistan Plans Caspian Naval Base," *Radio Free Europe Radio Liberty*, August 31, 2009, available from *www.rferl.org/content/Turkmenistan_Plans_Caspian_Naval_Base/1811441.html.*

98. *Ibid.*

99. Marlene Laruelle and Sebastien Peyrouse, "The Militarisation of the Caspian Sea: 'Great Games' and 'Small Games' over the Caspian Fleets," *China and Eurasia Forum Quarterly*, Vol. 7, No. 2, 2009, p. 25.

100. Binnie.

101. Nasser Karimi, "Jamaran-2, Iran Destroyer, Launched In The Caspian Sea," *Huffington Post*, March 17, 2013, available from *www.huffingtonpost.com/2013/03/17/jamaran-2-destroyer-iran-caspian-sea_n_2895553.html.*

102. "Iran launches indigenous Jamaran 2 destroyer in Caspian Sea," March 17, 2013, available from *www.presstv.com/detail/2013/03/17/294010/iran-launches-jamaran-2-destroyer/.*

103. Christopher Harmer, "Iranian Naval and Maritime Strategy," *Middle East Security Report 12*, Washington, DC: Institute for the Study of War, June 2013, p. 16.

104. *Ibid.*

105. Binnie.

106. BBC Monitoring, Interfax-AVN military news agency, Moscow, Russia, 1305GMT, November 6, 2012.

107. "Iranian naval group docked in Astrakhan carries message of peace, envoy says," PressTV, June 28, 2013, available from *www.presstv.com/detail/2013/06/28/311292/iran-naval-group-carries-message-of-peace/*. The Iranian port call to Astrakhan followed the docking of a Russian naval group (which included the *Admiral Panteleyev*, an anti-submarine destroyer, and two logistic battleships, the *Peresvet* and the *Admiral Nevelskoi*, with a combined crew of 712) at the southern Iranian port of Bandar Abbas in April 2013.

108. Vladimir Putin, "Presidential Address to the Federal Assembly," December 12, 2013, available from *eng.kremlin.ru/news/6402*.

109. Jahangir Karami, "The Collective Security System in the Caspian Sea. Opportunities, Restrictions and Future Perspective," *Caspian Factor*, London, UK: Institute for Caspian Cooperation, May 30, 2013.

110. Quoted in Pivovar, p. 137.

111. "Work on Caspian Sea Draft Convention Progressing," *Azernews*, November 25, 2013, available from *www.azernews.az/azerbaijan/61886.html*.

112. *Ibid.*

113. Karami.

114. "Caspian states adopt declaration on repelling aggressors," *RIA Novosti*, October 16, 2007, available from *en.rian.ru/world/20071016/84185487.html*.

115. *Ibid.*

116. *Ibid.*

117. Panfilova.

118. *Ibid.*

119. *Ibid.*

120. The CSTO collective peacekeeping force was established in 2007 and entered into force in 2009 with a total of 4,000 personnel. BBC Monitoring, Interfax-AVN military news agency, Moscow, Russia, 1026GMT, October 3, 2012.

U.S. ARMY WAR COLLEGE

Major General William E. Rapp
Commandant

*****

STRATEGIC STUDIES INSTITUTE
and
U.S. ARMY WAR COLLEGE PRESS

Director
Professor Douglas C. Lovelace, Jr.

Director of Research
Dr. Steven K. Metz

Author
Dr. Tracey German

Editor for Production
Dr. James G. Pierce

Publications Assistant
Ms. Rita A. Rummel

*****

Composition
Mrs. Jennifer E. Nevil